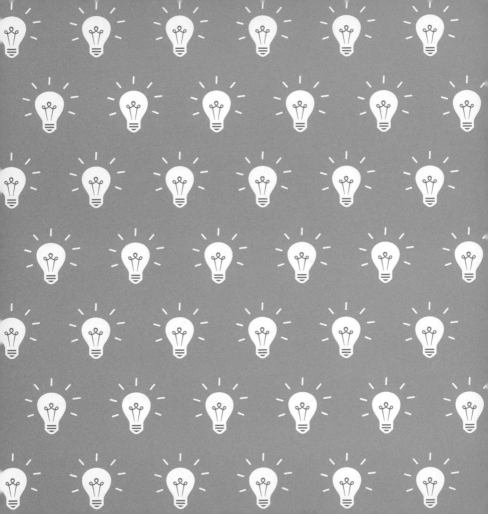

KNOWLEDGE

STUFF YOU OUGHT TO KNOW

RAY HAMILTON

summersdale

KNOWLEDGE

Summersdale Publishers Ltd
46 West Street
Chichester
West Sussex
PO19 1RP
UK

www.summersdale.com

Printed and bound in the Czech Republic

ISBN: 978-1-84953-889-3

Substantial discounts on bulk quantities of Summersdale books are available to corporations, professional associations and other organisations. For details contact Nicky Douglas by telephone: +44 (0) 1243 756902, fax: +44 (0) 1243 786300 or email: nicky@summersdale.com.

Disclaimer
All facts are correct to the best of the author's knowledge at the time of going to press. Statistics relating to populations and the like, particularly at a global or national level, are by their very nature fluid (it is very difficult to get populations to stand still long enough to be counted) and vary according to which statistician applied which method of counting on which day of the week. In any event, the author has done his best to pin these down to the extent necessary to at least compare different parts of the world.

For Joe Sandford

OTHER BOOKS BY RAY HAMILTON (ALL PUBLISHED BY SUMMERSDALE):

M25: A Circular Tour of the London Orbital (2015)

Trains: A Miscellany (2015)

The Joy of Golf: For Those Who Love the Fairway (2014)

The Joy of Cycling: For Those Who Love to Ride (2013)

Le Tour de France: The Greatest Race in Cycling History (2013)

Military Quotations: Stirring Words of War and Peace (2012)

CONTENTS

ACKNOWLEDGEMENTS

My thanks to Summersdale Publishers for the opportunity to write this fun book and to Debbie Chapman in particular for her exceedingly helpful input and for being such a pleasure to work with again. Thanks also to my lovely wife Karen for first-reading everything I write, however painful that might be.

As this book is all about knowing stuff, I would like to acknowledge (alphabetically) my fellow members of the Ever Hopefuls quiz team at the splendid Rose and Crown pub in Mayfield, East Sussex: Chris Bryce, John (of) Gaunt, Jeanette Hore (our illustrious captain), David Howroyd and Steve Sandford. Without each and every one of you, this book would have been entirely possible.

My thanks also to Bob and Grace Bryan of Newtown, Pennsylvania, who did their best to drown me in the shallow end while I was trying to finish this book in Key West, Florida.

INTRODUCTION

This book is full of stuff that will make you sound much cleverer than you are, because the people who don't read this book won't know what's in it and you will. It will also help you understand what other people are talking about because you 'came across' something about it before (only in this book, I know, but they don't need to know that). At the very least, the knowledge you get from reading this book will allow you to nod more when other people say stuff.

It's not just your image and self-esteem that will benefit, though, because you actually need to know stuff for lots of other reasons as well. For example, you should know when scientists think the Maldives might disappear under the ever-rising sea levels of the Indian Ocean – imagine how rubbish your holiday would be if you had nowhere to stand?

You should know that Brad Pitt injured his Achilles tendon while playing the part of Achilles in the film *Troy*, thereby delaying production for several weeks, because it enhances your sense of irony to know something like that.

You should know that the computing power of your mobile phone is greater than that used to guide Apollo 11 to the surface of the moon and back in 1969, bcos it might make u appreciate ur phone a bit more 2 know that. LOL.

If being happy is important to you, you should definitely know that Denmark is regularly voted the happiest country in the world. If you can't go and live there, you should maybe at least go there for a holiday. Just for a laugh.

If you're fed up being the weak link in your pub quiz team, it will do no harm to know why only one runner out of 5,000 starters finished the Marathon of the North in 2013, what the biggest-selling book of all time is, how Julius Caesar managed a batting average of 15.78 for Surrey, whether there's a Guinness World Record for drinking Guinness and what were the contents of the first ever Twitter tweet. I could go on.

In fact, I will go on, because I just remembered I'm going to write a whole book about this stuff. It's going to be random, people.

*You cannot open a book
without learning something.*

Confucius

THE AMAZING GLOBE WE LIVE ON

INTRODUCTION

When people say the world is getting smaller, they have a point in the sense that it is increasingly easy to travel around much of it, but it is not becoming any less magnificent or diverse and you would still be hard pushed to see all it has to offer in a single lifetime. This chapter will take you on a whistle-stop tour that may just help you decide which bits of which continents should be at the top of your own bucket list. Bon voyage!

THE WORLD

Introductory stuff

On the one-third of the world that isn't covered by the world's five great oceans, nature has carved five continents and the human race has divided itself across those continents into around 200 countries. Before we look at those individual continents and oceans, let's remind ourselves of some proper global stuff.

Basic stuff

Circumference: 24,901 miles (40,075 km) at the equator
Largest continent: Asia
Largest ocean: Pacific
Highest mountain: Mount Everest (Tibet/Nepal, 8,850 metres/29,035 ft)
Lowest point: Dead Sea (Israel/Jordan, 429 metres/1,407 ft below sea level)

Longest river: Nile (4,258 miles/6,853 km)
Largest lake: Caspian Sea
Largest island: Greenland
Largest desert: Antarctic
Largest hot desert: Sahara

Other stuff

Earth is orbiting the sun at about 67,000 mph (108,000 km/h), so either trust in gravity or hold on to something just in case.

At the equator, the world is spinning on its axis at 1,040 mph (1,675 km/h), whereas at the poles it is hardly spinning at all. If you're reading this somewhere in the British Isles, you're rotating at about 600 mph (966 km/h).

Mount Everest is the highest mountain above sea level in the world, but Mount Chimborazo in Ecuador reaches further towards space because it is situated on the earth's equatorial bulge, making it the furthest point from the centre of the earth.

The Caspian Sea, which is the size of Japan, is the world's largest lake, and it takes five countries to surround it (Russia, Kazakhstan, Turkmenistan, Iran and Azerbaijan).

Lake Baikal in Russia is the world's oldest and deepest lake, holding 20 per cent of the world's fresh water.

In terms of quantity produced, the main crop in the world is sugarcane (produced mostly in Brazil, then India), followed by maize (USA, then China) and rice (China, then India).

It is estimated that two-thirds of the people in the world have never seen snow.

Natural phenomena like hurricanes swirl clockwise in the southern hemisphere and anticlockwise in the northern hemisphere. It is a myth that water swirls differently down a plughole on either side of the equator, though, whatever sales pitch you might be given by the equatorial locals who earn a living by charging tourists to see it happen before their eyes.

The prime meridian line that separates the western and eastern hemispheres at 0° longitude passes through eight countries as it runs up and down between the North and South Poles, three in Europe and five in Africa (it passes through no countries in the southern hemisphere):

1. United Kingdom
2. France
3. Spain
4. Algeria
5. Mali
6. Burkina Faso
7. Togo
8. Ghana

The 180th meridian, also known as the antimeridian, is the line that runs up and down between the poles on the other side of the world at 180° longitude to complete the circle started by the prime meridian line on the Greenwich side of the world. It is the meridian used, for the most part, as the International Date Line. It only touches land to cross the north-eastern tip of Russia, three Fijian islands and the Ross Dependency (claimed by New Zealand) on Antarctica. For the rest of the time it just runs up and down the vast Pacific Ocean, unloved and unnoticed except when crossed by ships. If you want to add a day to your life, always choose a cruise ship that will cross the line heading east. If you want to add a year to your life, choose a cruise ship that will cross it going east on your birthday, which can then be skipped entirely.

The equator passes through 13 countries, three in South America, seven in Africa, two in Asia and one in Australasia/Oceania:

1. Ecuador
2. Colombia
3. Brazil
4. São Tomé and Príncipe
5. Gabon
6. Republic of the Congo
7. Democratic Republic of the Congo
8. Uganda
9. Kenya
10. Somalia
11. The Maldives
12. Indonesia
13. Kiribati

STUFF AND NONSENSE

Keeping countries in line

The equator doesn't touch land as it passes through the Maldives in the Indian Ocean, or as it passes through Kiribati in the Pacific Ocean. It possibly tickles one of the smaller Kiribati islands at low tide, depending on who you listen to, but the archipelago has another claim to fame in any event. It is the only territory to straddle both the equator and the International Date Line. This places Kiribati in all four of the world's hemispheres and makes it the most geographically central territory in the world. Where the equator and the prime meridian meet on the other side of the world, in the Gulf of Guinea below West Africa (which is where your skewer would come out if you stuck it straight through a globe from Kiribati), there is no territory to compete for the title of most geographically central, leaving Kiribati the uncontested champion in this regard.

The rough horseshoe shape that outlines the perimeter of the vast Pacific Ocean (roughly speaking, it sweeps up from New Zealand, taking in Indonesia, the Philippines and Japan before skipping across from Siberia to Alaska and then running back down the western side of the Americas to the bottom of Chile) is known as the Ring of Fire on account of the large number of earthquakes and volcanic eruptions that take place along its 25,000-mile (40,000-km) length. It plays host to 452 volcanoes – over

75 per cent of the total number on earth – and experiences about 90 per cent of the world's earthquakes.

World religions

When it comes to faith, the peoples of the world believe vastly different things. The Hindu religion has a vast pantheon of gods in their many reincarnations and avatars, whereas those with a single god include Islam, Sikhism, Judaism and Christianity. Many Chinese and African traditional religions believe in the forces of nature and the influence of ancestral spirits, whilst Buddhism focuses on personal spiritual development, the Bahá'í faith emphasises the unity of mankind and its various faiths, and Spiritism concerns itself with our relationship with the spirits beyond.

Here are the main religions in order of the size of their followings:

1. Christianity   2.2 billion
2. Islam   1.6 billion
3. Hinduism   1 billion
4. Chinese traditional   394 million
5. Buddhism   376 million
6. African traditional   100 million
7. Sikhism   23 million
8. Spiritism   15 million
9. Judaism   14 million
10. Bahá'í   7 million
11. Jainism   4.2 million

Note: the world's secular community of atheists, agnostics and 'don't cares', including those who state 'no religious preference' on their census forms, is around 1.1 billion, putting non-believers in third place behind Christians and Islamists.

The seven continents

Strictly speaking, there are five continents because Europe and Asia are joined at the geological hip, and so are North and South America, but we'll treat them all as separate for the same reason that most people do: namely that they are very different from one another. There is much confusion also about the nomenclature of Australia/Australasia/Oceania, which we will deal with when we get to that chapter. Here are the seven 'continents' in the (alphabetical) order we are going to look at them in:

Continent	Countries	Population	Percentage of landmass
Africa	54	1.1 billion	20 per cent
Antarctica	0	5,000	9 per cent
Asia	45	4.2 billion	30 per cent

Australasia/ Oceania	14	29 million	5 per cent
Europe	49	742 million	7 per cent
North America	23	542 million	17 per cent
South America	13	393 million	12 per cent

The number of countries on each continent depends on the political view of whoever is doing the counting, but there are 193 member countries in the United Nations, plus a few would-be members, like Greenland, Kosovo, Palestine, Taiwan, The Vatican and Western Sahara. For the time being, the best they can hope for is observer status, which means being allowed in to watch. Of the would-be members, only Palestine and the Vatican currently enjoy observer status.

Five countries straddle Europe and Asia and have been included under both in the above table. They are Azerbaijan, Kazakhstan, Georgia, Russia and Turkey.

Egypt has been counted under Africa only, notwithstanding that it pokes into Asia by means of the Sinai Peninsula.

STUFF AND NONSENSE

Country file

Following the 'No' vote for Scottish independence in 2014, South Sudan remains the world's newest country and Juba the world's newest capital city. There is, however, a growing trend for self-declared countries, like Enclava on the border between Slovenia and Croatia. It is the size of a suburban garden and was claimed by some Poles who discovered that it sat on no man's land. Several thousand people have applied for citizenship and they have been offered a choice of five official languages: Polish, Slovenian, Croatian, English and Mandarin.

Most populous places

China is the world's most populous nation, with around 1.37 billion citizens. India is a relatively close second, with around 1.28 billion, and the USA is a very poor third, with just around 323 million. The most populous cities in the world are, according to United Nations figures and definition of 'urban area population':

1. Tokyo, Japan   37.8 million
2. Jakarta, Indonesia   30.5 million
3. Karachi, Pakistan   25.4 million

4.	Delhi, India	24.9 million
5.	Shanghai, China	23.4 million
6.	Beijing, China	21.0 million
7.	New York, USA	20.6 million
8.	Guangzhou, China	20.5 million
9.	São Paolo, Brazil	20.3 million
10.	Cairo, Egypt	18.3 million
11.	Mumbai, India	17.7 million
12.	Osaka, Japan	17.4 million

AFRICA

Introductory stuff

Africa is the continent with the most countries and the second-largest landmass and population. The Sahara desert separates the largely Arabic countries of North Africa from the sub-Saharan countries to the south. The countries of North Africa have more in common with the countries of the Middle East than they have with the rest of Africa, and Arabic is in fact the commonest language on the African continent, followed by English and Swahili. Islam is the commonest religion, followed by Christianity.

Basic stuff

Most populous city: Cairo (Egypt)
Largest country: Algeria

Highest point: Mount Kilimanjaro (Tanzania, 5,895 metres/19,340 ft)
Longest river: River Nile
Largest lake: Lake Victoria (Tanzania/Uganda/Kenya)
Highest waterfall: Tugela Falls, KwaZulu-Natal (South Africa)
Largest island: Madagascar (Indian Ocean)

Places to put on your bucket list:

1. Victoria Falls (Zimbabwe/Zambia)
2. Kruger National Park (South Africa)
3. Cape Town (South Africa)
4. Masai Mara National Reserve (Kenya)
5. Serengeti National Park (Tanzania)
6. Mount Kilimanjaro (Tanzania)
7. The pyramids of Giza (Egypt)
8. The islands of Mauritius, Zanzibar and Madagascar
9. Okavango Delta (Botswana)
10. Djemaa el-Fna (the main square in Marrakech, Morocco)
11. The rock-hewn churches of Lalibela (Ethiopia)

Other stuff

The continent is considered to be the birthplace of mankind, as the oldest fossils of *Homo sapiens* have been found in Ethiopia.

Because it reaches up 5,895 metres (19,340 ft), ice and snow can be seen on the top of Mount Kilimanjaro in spite of its proximity to the equator.

The River Nile has original sources in 11 different countries, but has just two main sources of supply, with Lake Victoria (Tanzania/Uganda/Kenya) feeding the White Nile and Lake Tana (Ethiopia) feeding the Blue Nile. The two Niles join forces near Khartoum (Sudan) before continuing their journey north to the Mediterranean.

Having flowed through ten other countries by the time it gets there, only 22 per cent of the River Nile runs through Egypt.

The African continent has the youngest population in the world, with around 50 per cent of people being under 20 years of age.

The number of people with access to the internet on the entire continent of Africa is lower than the population of Berlin or Madrid.

China is Africa's top trading partner and over a million Chinese citizens are living and working on the African continent.

The world's most isolated tree used to be the Ténéré Tree in the Sahara Desert, being the only tree for 250 miles in any direction. In 1973, despite it being so isolated, a drunk Libyan truck driver knocked it down and killed it.

ANTARCTICA

Introductory stuff

The vast ice-covered landmass at the bottom of the world is known mostly
for having the South Pole at its centre. Only a few scientists live there and
the small number of tourists who visit each year have to wrap up warm so
that they don't die. Antarctica's nearest neighbour is South America, but you
can't pop next door to borrow a cup of sugar without spending thousands
of dollars on a flight or a long boat journey. If you choose to borrow your
sugar by boat, your journey will include a couple of days chucking up over
the side as you cross the rough waters of the Drake Passage. Sugar is bad
for you anyway.

Basic stuff

There isn't much basic stuff, although it does at least have a highest point,
which is the 4,897-metre (16,066-ft) Vinson Massif, and it is, surprisingly,
the world's largest desert, because it hardly ever rains or snows. It's too
busy freezing.

Other stuff

The word Antarctica originally derives from the Greek word for 'opposite
to the north'.

The continent has no countries or governments, just the Antarctic Treaty of 1961, which declares international cooperation and peace to be mandatory.

If you want to look at one of the few websites registered in Antarctica, the TLD (top level domain) to use is .aq.

The sun rises once at the beginning of summer and sets once at the beginning of winter, thereby rendering itself invisible for the entire six months of winter and offering 24/7 sunbathing throughout the six months of summer (but you still can't sunbathe in summer and expect your extremities to be intact when you return to base).

The ice that covers Antarctica averages around a mile (1.6 km) in thickness and can be up to three miles (4.8 km) thick.

Doctors overwintering in Antarctica are advised to first have their appendix removed because it's difficult to operate on yourself if you're the only doctor around, although one Russian doctor did exactly that in 1961, using local anaesthetic, a mirror and two expeditioners to operate the surgical retractors.

At the McMurdo Scientific Research Station on Ross Island, there is an ATM and you can attend aerobics and yoga classes.

In 2013 the American heavy metal band Metallica played a silent gig inside a dome at the Argentine Antarctic Base, with all 120 members of the audience hearing the music through headphones to avoid environmentally unfriendly noise amplification.

ASIA

Introductory stuff

With 60 per cent of the world's population spread across 30 per cent of the world's landmass, including many of the most populous cities in the world, Asia is big. From Arctic Siberia to the Arabian Desert, from the Himalayas to the low-lying Maldives, the continent encompasses pretty much every environment known to mankind.

Basic stuff

Most populous city: Tokyo (Japan)
Largest country: Russia
Highest point: Mount Everest (Tibet/Nepal, 8,850 metres/29,035 ft)
Longest river: Cháng Jiāng, aka Yangtze (China)
Largest lake: Caspian Sea
Highest waterfall: Hannoki-no-taki (Japan)
Largest island: Borneo

Places to put on your bucket list:

1. Great Wall of China
2. Terracotta Army (Xi'an, China)
3. Hong Kong
4. Singapore
5. Taj Mahal (Agra, India)
6. Angkor Wat temple (Siem Reap, Cambodia)
7. The Rose City of Petra (Jordan)
8. The temples and gardens of Kyoto (Japan)
9. The island of Bali (Indonesia)
10. The city of Kuala Lumpur (Malaysia)
11. Ha Long Bay (Vietnam)

Other stuff

Nine out of ten of the world's tallest buildings are in Asia. The Burj Khalifa in Dubai, UAE, is currently the tallest at 828 metres (2,717 ft), but it is due to be surpassed in around 2020 by the Jeddah Tower in Saudi Arabia, which will be a whole kilometre (3,280 ft) tall.

The New South China Mall in Dongguan, China, is the largest in the world by a huge margin, but 99 per cent of it has lain empty since it opened in 2005.

Mandarin Chinese is the world's most widely spoken language, with over a billion speakers.

In Vietnam everybody has the same 'birthday'. Their actual day of birth is not acknowledged, and instead everybody turns a year older on the day of the Vietnamese New Year, called Tết.

The Chinese New Year is responsible for the largest human migration on earth each year. In 2016, almost 3 billion people undertook journeys home by plane, train, car, motorcycle and bicycle.

Thanks to the regularity of the monsoon rains, China is the world's biggest producer of rice and tea, followed by India in both cases.

The Metabo Law in Japan requires everyone between the ages of 40 and 75 to have their waist measured by a representative of the Japanese government. Anything over 85 cm (33.5 in) for men and 90 cm (35.5 in) for women requires corrective measures. I assume Sumo wrestlers are exempt.

The North Korean calendar year begins on 15 April, the birthday of its founding member Kim Il-sung.

Over 4,000 children in China have been named 'Olympic Games' (Aoyun).

There are over 200 corpses on Mount Everest, some of which are used as waypoints for climbers.

The mango is the national fruit of India, Pakistan and the Philippines, and is the national tree of Bangladesh. India is the world's largest producer of the mango.

You can buy cans of fresh air in China, including cans of Canadian, Australian, Tibetan and Taiwanese air. If one of your mates slipped you a can of Beijing air for a laugh, you would not be well pleased.

The Maldives are only on average 1.2 metres (4 ft) above the waters of the Indian Ocean and scientists think the island republic might disappear altogether within 60 years.

Whenever there is a poor vanilla bean harvest on Madagascar or Indonesia, the world's dominant producers, the price of vanilla ice cream soars accordingly.

AUSTRALASIA/OCEANIA

Introductory stuff

The vast region of Oceania comprises Australia plus the 25,000 volcanic or coral islands of the Pacific Ocean that make up the 15 nations of the Micronesia, Melanesia and Polynesia island groups, including New Zealand and Papua New Guinea. Geographically speaking, Oceania also contains a bunch of dependencies, including Christmas Island (Australia), Hawaii (USA), the Pitcairn Islands (UK) and Rapa Nui, aka Easter Island (Chile).

The unofficial term Australasia causes much confusion. Some use it to refer to Australia and New Zealand only, while others use it to refer to Australia, New Zealand and New Guinea, but mostly it is now used interchangeably with Oceania, which is even less helpful.

The continent of Australia is easier to define, because it has been shaped by the shifting of tectonic plates within the earth's crust. It comprises the mainland of Australia plus the nearby islands of Tasmania, New Guinea, Seram and Timor.

Basic stuff

Most populous city: Sydney (Australia)
Largest country: Australia
Highest point: Mount Wilhelm (Papua New Guinea, 4,509 metres/14,794 ft)
Longest river: Murray River, Australia
Largest lake: Lake Eyre, Australia
Highest waterfall: Browne Falls, New Zealand
Largest island: New Guinea

Places to put on your bucket list:

1. Uluru/Ayers Rock (Australia)
2. Great Barrier Reef (Australia)
3. Sydney Harbour Bridge (Australia)
4. Kangaroo Island (Australia)
5. New Zealand (especially South Island)
6. Rapa Nui, aka Easter Island (Polynesia)
7. Tahiti (Polynesia)
8. Bora Bora (Polynesia)
9. Fiji (Melanesia)
10. Hawaii (USA)

Other stuff

The Great Barrier Reef is the largest structure composed of living things in the world (because a reef is made up of living coral). A UNESCO World Heritage Site, the marine park stretches about 1,800 miles (3,000 km) alongside the coast of Queensland in north-east Australia and the reef is the only living thing on earth visible from space.

New Zealand is so breathtakingly beautiful that it positively starred as Middle-earth in *The Lord of the Rings* trilogy. The Shire village of Hobbiton was created in the farming area of Matamata on North Island.

The moai, the 887 giant statues of human figures on Rapa Nui/Easter Island, were once believed by the islanders to be the living faces of ancestors, but in recent years their true purpose has finally been discovered – an opportunity for tourists to take loads of selfies. It was looking them in the face all along.

Going walkabout in the Australian bush was originally a rite of passage for an adolescent Aboriginal male to prove himself capable of surviving in the wild away from his family.

The pre-game haka performed by the All Blacks, the New Zealand rugby team, was originally performed as a Māori war dance intended to intimidate an enemy prior to the commencement of battle. In other words, for exactly the same reason the All Blacks perform it now.

Kangaroo Island, which lies just off the south coast of Australia near Adelaide, is a great place to spot penguins, sea lions, koalas, pelicans, echidnas, possums, bandicoots and (go on, have a guess) kangaroos.

The island of New Guinea is the second largest in the world (after Greenland). Its western half is part of Indonesia and its eastern half, Papua New Guinea, gained independence from Australia in 1975. According to the UN at least (scientists take a different ecogeographical view of such matters), this places the Indonesian bit of the island within Asia and the Papua New Guinea bit within Australasia/Oceania.

Island nations

Leaving Australia aside for the moment, Oceania is made up of the following island nations:

Micronesia

1.   Federated States of Micronesia
2.   Kiribati
3.   Marshall Islands
4.   Nauru
5.   Palau

Melanesia

1.   Fiji
2.   Papua New Guinea
3.   Solomon Islands
4.   Vanuatu

Polynesia

1.   Cook Islands
2.   Niue
3.   New Zealand
4.   Samoa
5.   Tonga
6.   Tuvalu

The island of Kiritimati (Christmas Island) in the Micronesian republic of Kiribati was the first place on earth to experience the new millennium after a unilateral realignment of the International Date Line by Kiribati in 1995 moved it west of the Date Line. Tonga, which would otherwise have been the first place to experience the new millennium, tried to complain, but it was always a day late in doing so.

Tonga became known as the Friendly Islands following the convivial welcome afforded to Captain James Cook when he first turned up there in 1773, although some historians believe that the chiefs wanted in fact to kill Cook but couldn't agree on how to go about it. Surely they should just have Cooked him.

Hawaii, the 50th State of the USA, is the remotest population centre on earth, its nearest neighbour being California, 2,390 miles (3,850 km) to the east.

Geologically speaking, Mauna Kea, on Hawaii's Big Island, is the tallest mountain on earth, standing at over 10,000 metres (33,000 ft) from its oceanic base to its relatively low height (4,207 metres/13,800 ft) above sea level. Mount Everest is 'only' 8,850 metres/29,035 ft from top to bottom.

New Zealand was the first country in the world to allow women to vote. Australia was the second.

Per capita, Australians spend more on gambling than any other nation, especially at the pokies (poker slot machines).

Melbourne has the largest Greek population of any city outside of Greece.

The Australian Alps in the south-east of the country receive more snowfall than Switzerland.

STUFF AND NONSENSE

Starbuck Island is a coral atoll in the central Pacific, uninhabited save for a colony of sooty terns and some green turtles. It therefore has no Starbuck's coffee shop. But there is, of course, a McDonald's. (I might have made that last bit up.)

EUROPE

Introductory stuff

Europe is what you might call diverse, with many different cultures and languages spread across 48 countries. From cool Scandinavia in the north to the sunny Mediterranean countries in the south, from the Atlantic coastline in the west to the Turkish delights of the east, the only thing these countries seem to have in common is that they share the same landmass. Except for the British Isles, of course, which don't even do that. Some of the countries even leave Europe after a while in order to spill into Asia, like Russia and Turkey. Russia does, however, still manage to be the largest country in Europe before combining with its Asian bit to become the largest country in the world. The geographic boundary between Europe and Asia is primarily formed by the Ural and Caucasus mountain ranges.

Basic stuff

Most populous city: Istanbul (Turkey)
Largest country: Russia
Highest point: Mount Elbrus (Ural Range, Russia/Georgia,
    5,642 metres/18,510 ft)
Longest river: Volga (Russia)
Largest lake: Lake Ladoga (Russia)
Highest waterfall: Vinnufossen (Norway)
Largest island: Great Britain

Places to put on your bucket list:

1. Eiffel Tower (Paris, France)
2. Château de Chenonceau (Loire Valley, France)
3. Grand Canal (Venice, Italy)
4. Colosseum (Rome, Italy)
5. Leaning Tower of Pisa (Italy)
6. Acropolis of Athens (Greece)

7. The basilica museum of Hagia Sophia (Istanbul, Turkey)
8. Red Square (Moscow, Russia)
9. The Hermitage Museum (St Petersburg, Russia)
10. Lake Bled (Slovenia)
11. Basílica of the Sagrada Família (Barcelona, Spain)
12. The prehistoric monument of Stonehenge (England)
13. The Lake District (England)
14. Scottish Highlands and Islands
15. Giant's Causeway (Northern Ireland)
16. Snowdonia (Wales)

European Union

Of the 49 nations that make up the continent of Europe, 28 at the time of writing are members of the EU – a confederation of states designed to foster cooperation on matters of law, human rights and democracy and facilitate trade and travel for its citizens. It started as the European Economic Community with just six members in 1957 (Belgium, France, West Germany, Italy, Luxembourg and the Netherlands) and an intermittent stream of new joiners has increased the numbers ever since, with Croatia the most recent to join in 2013. A number of other countries are keen to join, while the UK electorate upset the apple cart somewhat by voting in favour of leaving the union in a referendum held on 23 June 2016.

Of the 28 EU members, nine opted out of the Eurozone in order to maintain their own individual currency: Bulgaria, Croatia, Czech Republic, Denmark, Hungary, Poland, Romania, Sweden and the UK. In contrast to this, four tiny countries that are not members of the EU have been allowed to join the Eurozone anyway: San Marino, Andorra, Monaco and Vatican City.

Bizarrely, the furthest points of the EU's territory are a third of the earth's circumference apart from one another, because the EU has a presence in the continents of South America, North America and Africa. This is because the Caribbean islands of Saint Martin, Guadeloupe and Martinique, the territory of French Guiana in South America and the islands of Réunion and Mayotte in the Indian Ocean off the coast of Africa are all part of France (as opposed to being dependencies).

If and when Turkey joins the EU, its territory will extend into Asia and this will leave Antarctica and Australasia/Oceania as the only continents without a presence in the EU (although Australia has been allowed into the Eurovision Song Contest recently, which is probably a lot cooler anyway).

Other stuff

Finland and the Scandinavian countries of Norway, Sweden and Denmark are regularly voted amongst the happiest places on earth to live (probably because they're the only people who can watch all the brilliant Scandi noir TV dramas without subtitles).

The place with the longest name in Europe (but not the world) is Llanfairpwllgwyngyllgogerychwyrndrobwllllantysiliogogogoch in Wales. It means 'The church of Saint Mary in the hollow of the white hazel near the fierce whirlpool and the church of Saint Tysilio of the red cave'. There is a place in New Zealand with 27 more letters than that, though.

An estimated one in ten Europeans is conceived in an IKEA bed.

The M25 orbital motorway round London is roughly equally divided between the eastern and western hemispheres of the world.

Civilians of Seville are called Sevillians.

Tromsø sits well inside the Arctic Circle at the top of Norway and has the northernmost just about everything in the world, including symphony orchestra, mosque, university, 18-hole golf course, aquarium, Burger King and vegetarian restaurant! If you're very lucky, you might also see the Northern Lights or the midnight sun while you're there.

The Sagrada Família church in Barcelona is taking longer to build than the pyramids of Egypt.

There are more doner kebab outlets in Berlin than in Istanbul.

The most visited places in Europe are Notre Dame cathedral in Paris, Disneyland to the east of Paris and the Grand Bazaar in Istanbul.

The escalators in London's underground system travel a distance twice the circumference of the world every week.

Brussels Airport sells more chocolate than any other single location in the world.

Many tourists still visit the Highlands of Scotland in the hope of catching sight of the Loch Ness Monster (except, of course, during the haggis season, when they go on haggis-hunting trips instead).

STUFF AND NONSENSE

Crazy European laws that remain valid today

1. In France it is against the law to call your pig Napoleon.
2. In Switzerland it is illegal to hang clothes, mow the lawn or wash the car on a Sunday.
3. In Italy a man can be arrested for wearing a skirt.
4. In Germany no one is considered to be legally drunk during Oktoberfest
5. In Greece it is illegal to wear heels or dance naked at ancient sites (so don't even think about dancing naked in heels at the Acropolis).
6. In the UK it is against the law to fall off the top of the Blackpool Tower, or to have sex under a pier while Morris dancing (the latter is quite a difficult thing to pull off in any event).

7. During the long hours of winter in Sweden, it is illegal to complain about the lack of light.
8. It is forbidden to urinate in a canal in the Netherlands unless you are pregnant.
9. In Portugal, it is illegal to urinate in the ocean (although I'm pretty sure that's not being policed to any great extent).
10. There is an EU directive that all rubber boots must be sold with a user's manual in 12 different languages.

STUFF AND NONSENSE

Big Ben grows up

Britain's highest mountain, Ben Nevis in the Scottish Highlands, used to stand proud at 1,344 metres. Now it stands even prouder, at 1,345 metres. That's because it has just been measured and rounded up using sophisticated satellite technology.

The last time it was measured, in 1949, surveyors spent 20 nights at the summit of the Ben with relatively rudimentary equipment. They took their readings on the three clear nights they got out of 20 (remember, this is Scotland we're talking about, and on the other 17 nights they probably just sat around being buffeted half to death by ice-cold winds). Their measurements have now been proved correct to within a few centimetres. Respect.

NORTH AMERICA

Introductory stuff

The continent of North America encompasses the USA, Mexico, Canada, Greenland, the countries of Central America and the many islands of the Caribbean. From its highest point in Alaska (Denali/Mount McKinley) to its lowest point in California (the Badwater Basin in Death Valley), and surrounded by the Arctic Ocean to the north, the Pacific Ocean to the west and the Atlantic Ocean to the east, it has a rich variety of climates.

Basic stuff

Most populous city: New York (USA)
Largest country: Canada
Highest point: Denali, formerly known as Mount McKinley (Alaska, USA, 6,190 metres/20,310 ft)
Longest river: Missouri River (USA)
Largest lake: Lake Superior (Canada/USA)
Highest waterfall: James Bruce Falls (Canada)
Largest island: Greenland

Places to put on your bucket list:

1. Statue of Liberty (New York, USA)
2. Golden Gate Bridge (San Francisco, USA)
3. Grand Canyon (Arizona, USA)
4. Mount Rushmore National Memorial (South Dakota, USA)
5. Lincoln Memorial (Washington, D.C., USA)
6. Yellowstone National Park (Wyoming/Montana/Idaho, USA)
7. Niagara Falls (New York, USA/Ontario, Canada)
8. Banff National Park (Alberta, Canada)
9. Mayan ruins of Chichén Itzá (Mexico)
10. Pyramids of Teotihuacán (Mexico)
11. Bioluminescent Bay (Puerto Rico)
12. Shirley Heights (Antigua)

The seven countries of Central America that provide the land bridge between North and South America, breached only by the Panama Canal, are as follows:

1. Belize
2. Guatemala
3. El Salvador
4. Honduras
5. Nicaragua
6. Costa Rica
7. Panama

Other stuff

Vancouver is regularly voted the best place to live in North America. This probably has something to do with its nearly 300 parks, beaches and gardens and the fact that you can sometimes ski, swim and whale-watch all on the same day.

The average toll to pass through the Panama Canal is US$54,000.

The Grand Canyon, which hosts the Colorado River through Arizona, is a mile deep and 277 miles (446 km) long.

Lake Superior is the world's largest freshwater lake by area and it holds more water than the other four Great Lakes (Huron, Michigan, Ontario and Erie) combined.

Chocolate was created in what is now Mexico. Ixcacao was the Mayan goddess of chocolate and the Aztecs believed that cacao seeds were a gift from the gods. The seeds were once considered so valuable (not least on account of their supposed aphrodisiac powers) that they were used as a form of currency.

The USA purchased Alaska (the 49th State) from Russia for US$7.2 million in 1867 and later named the capital Juneau after the first man (Joe Juneau) to discover gold there in 1880.

A colony of almost 50,000 quaking aspen tree trunks in the Wasatch Mountains of Utah, USA, has been shown to be entirely cloned from a single underground root system, making it the largest single organism in the world. Nicknamed Pando (Latin for 'I spread'), it is also known as the Trembling Giant. It is thought to be around 80,000 years old.

There are more churches per square mile in Jamaica than in any other country in the world.

Native American tribes got saddled with being called Indians because Christopher Columbus thought he had sailed all the way round to Asia (the Indies) when he arrived in 1492. The islands of the Caribbean were promptly renamed the West Indies to distinguish them from the real (East) Indies.

The USA has overtaken Russia and Saudi Arabia in the last couple of years to become the world's largest producer of oil and gas.

There are more than 50 million native Spanish speakers in the USA (more than there are in Spain), including 47 per cent of New Mexicans and 6 per cent of Alaskans.

The USA has no official language.

Around one in five Canadians have French as their mother tongue.

The comparatively tiny country of Guatemala is the fourth most populous nation in North America, after the USA, Mexico and Canada.

Polls regularly claim that many Americans believe that not a single moon landing has taken place and that the first moon landing in particular was faked to win the 'space race' with the USSR.

STUFF AND NONSENSE

Famous Canadians

Here are some famous Canadians you probably thought were Americans if you didn't know they were Canadians:

1. Justin Bieber (singer)
2. Keanu Reeves (actor/director)
3. Jim Carrey (comedian/actor)
4. Avril Lavigne (singer/songwriter)
5. Leslie Nielsen (actor)
6. Leslie Nielsen's brother, Erik (ex-Deputy Prime Minister of Canada, in fact)
7. Kiefer Sutherland (actor)
8. Neil Young (singer/songwriter)
9. Ryan Gosling (actor)
10. Michael J. Fox (actor)
11. William Shatner (actor)
12. Céline Dion (singer)

Note: Michael J. Fox's middle name is Andrew.

SOUTH AMERICA

Introductory stuff

From the Atacama Desert to the Amazonian rainforest, from tiny Dutch-speaking Suriname to huge Portuguese-speaking Brazil, South America is a continent of contrasts. It contains a number of the world's superlatives, including highest waterfall (Angel Falls), longest mountain range (Andes), largest river basin (Amazon) and driest (non-polar) place on earth (Atacama Desert). It is a legacy of European colonisation that Spanish and Portuguese remain the main languages and that Roman Catholicism remains the main religion across South America.

Basic stuff

Most populous city: São Paolo (Brazil)
Largest country: Brazil
Highest point: Aconcagua (Andes Range, Argentina, 6,960 metres/22,838 ft)
Longest river: Amazon
Largest lake: Lake Titicaca (Bolivia/Peru)
Highest waterfall: Angel Falls (Venezuela)
Largest island: Isla Grande de Tierra del Fuego (Argentina/Chile)

Places to put on your bucket list:

1.   Christ the Redeemer (Rio de Janeiro, Brazil)

2. Machu Picchu (Peru)
3. Torres del Paine National Park (Chile)
4. Galápagos Islands (Ecuador)
5. Iguazu Falls (Argentina/Brazil)
6. Angel Falls (Venezuela)
7. Tropical wetlands of the Pantanal (Brazil/Paraguay/Bolivia)
8. Buenos Aires (Argentina)
9. Salar de Uyuni salt flat (Bolivia)

Other stuff

Although South America is largely inhabited by Spanish and Portuguese speakers, the Quechuan language and culture remain strong in the central Andean region, including in Colombia, Ecuador, Peru, Bolivia, Chile and Argentina. Quechuan is still being spoken by over ten million people in these six countries.

The indigenous culture and language of the Guaraní in the southern half of the continent is also hanging in there, having barely survived European colonisation, slavery, the Inquisition and any number of European diseases.

Chile is the skinniest vertical-running country on the planet, stretching north–south for 2,653 miles (4,270 km). Dominated by the Andes, the world's longest mountain range, its climate zones include subtropical, Mediterranean, desert, alpine, tundra and glacial.

The 38-metre-tall (125-ft-tall) art deco statue of Christ the Redeemer atop Corcovado mountain in Rio de Janeiro has been damaged twice by lightning strikes, in 2008 (causing damage to the head, eyebrows and some fingers) and again in 2014 (just a dislodged finger this time).

Machu Picchu is a dry-stone citadel of the Incan Empire high up in the Cusco region of Peru, mysteriously abandoned in the sixteenth century and rediscovered by American college professor Hiram Bingham while out trekking in 1911.

Famous for their unique marine ecology and wildlife, the volcanic Galápagos Islands straddle the equator in the Pacific Ocean, 600 miles (973 km) west of their parent country Ecuador. Their provincial capital is Puerto Baquerizo Moreno on San Cristóbal, the nearest island to mainland Ecuador.

Of the 13 countries that straddle the equator around the world, Ecuador is the only one to have been given its name (in Spanish).

Angel Falls on the Orinoco river in Venezuela constitute the highest uninterrupted waterfall on earth. Surprisingly, they are named after Jimmie Angel, the American aviator who first flew over them. His ashes were scattered over the falls after he died.

Paraguay and Bolivia are the only two landlocked countries on the entire continent. Running clockwise from the bottom, the other eleven that hug some coastline or other are:

1. Chile
2. Peru
3. Ecuador
4. Colombia
5. Venezuela
6. Guyana
7. Suriname
8. France
9. Brazil
10. Uruguay
11. Argentina

That's right, France, because apparently, as we have already seen, French Guiana is still considered by the French to be inside the country of France.

The city of Ushuaia in the Argentinian part of Isla Grande de Tierra del Fuego is the southernmost city on earth and has the world's southernmost ski resort, golf course and Irish pub.

THE NATURAL ORDER OF THINGS WE SHARE THE GLOBE WITH

INTRODUCTION

There are many weird and wonderful creatures on planet earth because they have had many weird and wonderful environments in which to evolve. They had to survive and adapt in their natural habitat or move on to find a more suitable one whenever climatic or environmental conditions went against them, which was generally fine if time was on their side.

Some weren't so lucky, like the dodo on Mauritius, which didn't have time to learn to fly before it was hunted to extinction by idiot humans. The blue whale knew what it was doing, though, taking its time to evolve in the largest hunting ground of all: the world's oceans. If it had decided to evolve in the forest, say, it probably wouldn't have had enough growing room to become the largest mammal in the world.

Many species continue to thrive around the world, others remain under threat from human intervention. In this chapter we're going to look at some of the more interesting creatures on earth, within the environments in which they live.

THINGS THAT SWIM

The five oceans of the world (Arctic, Atlantic, Indian, Pacific and Southern/Antarctic) are in reality one large connected body of water, which also includes the hundreds of shallower seas closer to land and the rivers that spill into those seas. All of this water combined forms two-thirds of the world's surface and plays host to millions of wet, slippery things. Penguins and seals are much happier living in the sea and do so for most of their lives, so I'm including them in this section, but they do have to come ashore to breed, moult and be inspected by David Attenborough, which is how we know so much about them.

The **blue whale** grows to a length of 30 metres and is probably the largest and heaviest animal to have ever existed. The only dinosaur that might have come close to it in size was the *Argentinosaurus*, but it's 97 million years since we spotted one of those. The blue whale is about three times the size of a *Tyrannosaurus rex* and its tongue alone can weigh as much as an elephant, and yet all it ever eats is tiny krill – although admittedly it does swallow a few tons at a time.

A **shark** can detect one part of blood in a million parts of water. Statistically, though, you are more likely to die from a falling coconut than a shark attack, so let's not over-worry the whole shark thing.

The male **emperor penguin** is as hard as nails, standing over the egg it has been left to incubate for over 60 days on Antarctica, one of the least hospitable spots on earth. It is constantly battered by freezing winds and doesn't get as much as a single fish to eat.

The **leopard seal**, so called on account of the spots on its underbelly, is second only to the killer whale among the predators of Antarctica. Its menu includes smaller seals and six different species of penguin: emperor, king, chinstrap, rockhopper, gentoo and Adélie.

The distinctive black-and-white **killer whale**, or orca, munches its way through pretty much everything it comes across in the world's oceans, including octopus, squid, dolphin, sea turtle, seal, penguin, other species of whale (even those larger than itself) and shark, including the great white. Given the chance, they will even prey on land-based animals, like reindeer swimming between islands.

Otters sleep holding hands while floating on their backs. I almost used the word cute there.

After feeding out at sea for up to four years, and in order to spawn the next generation, large populations of **Atlantic salmon** return upstream (and quite often uphill) to their birthplace in the rivers that flow into the north Atlantic and, due to human introduction, the north Pacific.

When it comes to attacking swimmers, the **box jellyfish** in Australia has an advantage over sharks and crocodiles – it is virtually transparent, which means you won't see it coming. As vinegar is the most effective treatment against its sting, many beaches in the country have 'vinegar posts' for you to run to. As the sting can be fatal, though, it might be safer to take your own bottle just in case (cue joke about well-endowed swimmers).

The red-bellied piranha of South America will eat anything, including cattle that stoop to have a drink in the wrong river at the wrong time. The piranhas have the nose and mouth as a starter and carry on from there.

The duck-billed platypus of Australia is very bad at being a mammal, because it lays eggs, hunts underwater and struggles to walk on land on account of its webbed feet.

The Great Barrier Reef off the coast of Australia supports huge numbers of whale, dolphin, porpoise, dugong (sea cow) and turtle, not to mention 1,500 species of fish and 215 species of birds. There are also saltwater crocodiles, sea snakes and 125 species of shark, so perhaps just go out on a glass-bottomed boat if you're of a nervous disposition.

FLYING THINGS

There are a number of advantages to being a bird. You can see further, swoop down on unsuspecting prey and move quickly on to the next plant, tree, field or bit of ocean when you've finished with the last one. If you're a tasty game bird, though, you do have to keep your ears open for gunshot.

As with creatures of the sea and land, there is no shortage of variety when it comes to our feathered friends.

The Arctic tern is a small elegant seabird that doesn't look like it's bred for stamina, but it undertakes the longest annual migration of any living bird, breeding in the Arctic and overwintering in the Antarctic. Its round trip of around 25,000 miles (40,000 km) allows it to spend more time in daylight than any other creature in the world.

The mighty sea eagle eats more lamb than fish. This makes perfect sense when you think about it, because lambs are rubbish at slithering away. They can have a bit of a gambol, it's true, but it's a gambol that doesn't always pay off when there's a sea eagle about.

The bee hummingbird of Cuba is the smallest bird in the world, not much bigger than a bumblebee and weighing less than a 1p coin. It hovers in order to feed itself, flapping its wings 80 times every second. Needing a lot of sugar energy to maintain this Herculean effort, it needs to lap up nectar at a rate of 13 licks per second.

The commonest bird in the world is the red-billed quelea, which belongs to the weaver family, but you're unlikely to have heard of it if you're not a farmer in sub-Saharan Africa. There are over a billion of the little blighters, and they swarm around in flocks up to two-million strong, devastating whole wheat fields like a plague of locusts in a matter of minutes.

The **wandering albatross** (also known as a goonie) wanders all over the southern polar region. With the widest wingspan of any living bird, up to 3.5 metres (11 ft) in some cases, it only has to flap its wings very occasionally to remain aloft. It would be very bad luck indeed to have this particular albatross around your neck.

A **frigatebird** looks like a pterodactyl as it glides across the skies of the tropics, but is probably better known for the huge bright-red sac displayed on the male's throat during the breeding season.

The birds of the Galápagos Islands have been famous since Charles Darwin concluded that the evolution of finches and mockingbirds had varied on different islands there, but the star attraction today is the **blue-footed booby**. It spears itself into the water at 60 mph (97 km/h) and consumes its catch while still underwater, leaving it free to concentrate on looking cool when it comes back up again.

The **laughing kookaburra**, the heaviest of the world's kingfishers, isn't really laughing when it calls – it's just marking out its territory.

STUFF AND NONSENSE

The rough-faced shag

There used to be just two types of shag in New Zealand and then some scientists decided they would like more shags, so they split the shags into bounty shags, Auckland shags, Stewart shags, Campbell shags, Chatham shags and rough-faced shags. This turned all the shags into endangered species, because their individual numbers dwindled dramatically upon receiving their new names. As if it wasn't bad enough for the rough-faced shags to be facing unexpected extinction, they also had to put up with being called rough-faced shags, so the scientists relented and said they could be called either king shags or rough-faced shags. I assume most of the shags opted to become king shags, but I like to think there are still a couple of rough-faced shags somewhere in New Zealand.

CREATURES OF THE LAND

For the obvious reasons that they can't swim off or fly to another part of the world, it is less easy for land animals to emigrate to another continent, which means you have to do a bit of travelling yourself if you want to see them in their natural habitat. It helps, therefore, to know which animals live where, so that you don't go to Antarctica to look for polar bears, for example.

Polar bears live up north within the Arctic circle, along with moose, caribou, musk ox and brilliant-white wolves and foxes. Conversely, if any of these Arctic animals ever clapped eyes on a penguin, the first thing they would probably say to it is, 'What the hell are you?'

The easiest continent on which to spot a quite astonishing array of animals is, of course, Africa, the safari destination of choice ever since Victorian explorers 'discovered' the continent, so let's start there.

Wildlife of Africa

The so-called Big Five that everyone hopes to see on safari are African lion, African elephant, African leopard, Cape buffalo and white or black rhinoceros. The shy leopard is the most elusive of the five, whereas the buffalo is statistically the one most likely to kill you.

East Africa hosts the largest wildlife migration on earth, with around a quarter of a million zebras joining around 1.5 million wildebeest each year from the Serengeti Plains of Tanzania to the Masai Mara in Kenya for their summer holiday. Around 200,000 of the migrating herds won't survive the arduous 1,800-mile round trip, owing to a combination of starvation, disease, overexertion and predation. Young calves are particularly vulnerable to the big cats, while crocodiles also look forward with relish to the unavoidable river crossings on the route.

Africa has the world's largest land animal (African elephant), tallest animal (giraffe), largest primate (gorilla) and fastest land animal (cheetah).

The hilarious sideways-dancing lemurs of Madagascar are among the world's most endangered species thanks to invasive logging and hunting.

The small, friendly-sounding honey badger will fight any other creature it comes across to the death, including lions, hyenas, leopards and pythons. It is the world's most fearless creature according to Guinness World Records, and the only one to have played in central defence for Millwall Football Club (I might have made that last bit up).

Down by the river, hippos kill more people than crocodiles do. Try not to get in their way, and try especially hard not to stand between them and their watering holes.

The aardvark might look like a cross between a kangaroo, a pig and a rabbit, and lick ants for a living, but there isn't a creature on earth that can beat it for position within the alphabet.

Wildlife of Asia

The giant pandas of central China are under threat from habitat loss and also because they are not very good at mating. The female giant panda is good to go only once a year for a couple of days, which means the male giant panda has to be quick off the mark, and that's not something he's exactly famous for.

Perhaps the most majestic of all living animals, the **tiger** is the national animal of Bangladesh, India, Malaysia and South Korea. If you're on the run from one, try not to dwell on the fact that they can run at up to 40 mph (64 km/h), swim for up to 20 miles (32 km) and leap over 5 metres (16 ft).

One hump or two? The **dromedary** is the single-humped camel that lives mostly in the Middle East and the Horn of Africa. The two-humped **Bactrian camel** is the one that lives in central Asia.

The **Komodo dragon** is the world's largest lizard, growing up to 3 metres (10 ft) in length and feasting on everything from snakes to water buffalo and wild horses. It got to be so big because for millions of years it has been the largest predator on the five Indonesian islands it inhabits (including, of course, Komodo), and because it can smell a dying animal from a range of almost six miles (9.5 km).

The world's longest snake is the **reticulated python** found in South East Asia. It can grow to a length of 6.5 metres (21.3 ft) – about the same as the three tallest NBA basketball players of the 2015–2016 season laid end to end. It gets its name from the reticulated (net-like) pattern of its scales.

It is pure coincidence that the **orangutan** on the vast island of Borneo is orange-coloured, because orangutan is in fact the Malay word for 'person of the forest'.

The weirdest, funniest, ugliest monkey in the world is the **proboscis monkey**, found only on Borneo. The Indonesians (who share Borneo with citizens of Brunei and Malaysia) call it the Dutch monkey, having considered their nineteenth-century Dutch colonisers to have had similarly large bellies and noses.

STUFF AND NONSENSE

Charmed, I'm sure!

When the **king cobra** stands up, looks you in the eye, flares open its hood and hisses like a growling dog, you're about to have a venom delivery, and it's not one you're going to survive. The good news is that the cobra probably won't bother you if you don't bother it in the first place. It's also as deaf as a post, so it will be more interested in your movements than in anything you might say to it, which means you can charm it into not biting you just by the shape and movement of the flute you should never leave home without if you're going to meet a cobra (when snake charmers play their flute facing a cobra, they only make the sound to entertain watching tourists).

Wildlife of Australasia & Oceania

A koala is not a bear. It's just a koala. Looking cuddly, munching eucalyptus leaves and sleeping constitute the entire lifestyle of this downright lazy marsupial, which never spends more than 10 minutes a day on full-bodied exertion.

The red kangaroo is the largest mammal in Australia, standing up to 2 metres (7 ft) tall on the ground and up to 20 metres (66 ft) tall on the tail of a Qantas A380 aircraft.

The Tasmanian devil is a small violent mammal with a large head and neck that account for 25 per cent of its body mass. Even dingoes give it a wide berth.

The little bilby is like a miniature kangaroo with a rat's face and long sticky-up ears. It is so popular that Australians give chocolate bilbies instead of chocolate bunnies at Easter.

The aggressive Sydney funnel-web is probably the deadliest spider in the world. The record time for its venom to kill a human victim is recorded as 15 minutes, although it can take up to three days. Given the choice, always ask for the quick-acting stuff, because the next three days are probably not going to be all that pleasant. An antivenom was made available in 1981, but survival still depends on getting to the antivenom in time, so maybe it's best not to go too far on your walkabout just in case.

The sedentary kiwi is the national animal of New Zealand and is so popular that the term is used to refer to the country's citizens as well as its rugby league team. New Zealanders even changed the name of the 'Chinese gooseberry' they produced to kiwi fruit so that people would know where it came from.

In 1932 the Australian army lost a war to emus. Having been called in to control the growing numbers of the flightless bird, they gave up after realising that emus could scatter in every direction quicker than they could fire at them.

Wildlife of the Americas

The grizzly bear of North America can stand as tall as 3 metres (10 ft) on its hind legs, but the largest brown bear of all is the Kodiak bear in Alaska. Grizzlies and Kodiaks both like a nice bit of fresh salmon for dinner and given the choice will take a young one while it is still rich in protein. Their favourite bits are the skin, brain and roe of the salmon, so there are quite often leftovers for the resident gulls, ravens and foxes to enjoy.

Capable of growing up to 4.5 metres (15 ft) in length, the largest reptile in North America is the American alligator, or *Alligator mississippiensis*, to give it its proper title (and you probably should if you come face to face with one). It is the official state reptile of Florida, which has a population of 1.25 million gators.

The **tapir** of South and Central America might look like a large pig with a short trunk, but it's related to the horse and the rhinoceros, so you might not want to call it a large pig with a small trunk to its face.

The **jaguar** of the Amazon Basin is so called from the Tupi–Guarani word *yaguar*, which means 'he who kills with one leap'. One leap plus one bite is usually all it takes to bring down and take the life out of anything that moves on land or water, including the alligator-like caiman (and you need a pretty powerful bite to pierce through the armour of a reptile).

The **green anaconda** of South America is the largest and longest snake in the Americas, growing up to 9 metres (30 ft) and weighing up to 227 kg (500 pounds), with the female of the species much bigger and deadlier than the male. They don't need venom, because they can swallow pigs, caimans and even jaguars whole. If you haven't figured it out yet, that means they could also swallow you whole if they put their mind to it.

The semi-aquatic **capybara** of South America is the world's largest, and probably cutest, rodent. Up to 60 cm (2 ft) tall and over 1.2 metres (4 ft) long, they are solid enough to weigh as much as an adult human. There are plenty of them, so they can afford to be eaten in large numbers by jaguars and anacondas and still thrive (except the ones caught by the jaguars and anacondas, which thrive very badly indeed).

Giant tortoises gave the Galápagos Islands of Ecuador their name, *galápago* being an old Spanish word for tortoise. The most famous *galápago* was Lonesome George, the last of the Pinta Island tortoises, who very slowly shuffled off his mortal coil in 2012 at the age of 100 (which is in fact relatively young for a giant tortoise, the oldest on record having lived on Tonga to the ripe old age of 188).

Wildlife of Europe

The teddy bears that have served our children so well for generations are alive and well in the marshy taiga of northern Finland and Russia (even if teddy bears did get their nickname after the US president Theodore 'Teddy' Roosevelt). The **Eurasian brown bear** looks just like a real teddy bear, although I suspect it may be less cuddly.

The wolverine of northern Europe (and northern Canada and Alaska) will eat or scavenge just about anything, which is why its binomial name is *Gulo gulo* (Latin for 'glutton glutton'). Looking like a cross between a skunk and a miniature bear, the wolverine looks nothing like Hugh Jackman, but it's every bit as ferocious as the character he plays.

The only primates living free on the European continent were humans until the **Barbary macaque** was introduced from Morocco to Gibraltar, where around 250 continue to thrive on the rock. It was mistakenly given the alternative name of 'Barbary ape' by early travellers to North Africa on account of having almost no tail, but it is in fact a monkey.

In the UK, the red squirrel remains under constant threat from the much plainer grey squirrel. Introduced from North America in the nineteenth century to satisfy the Victorians' desire to enjoy different species of fauna and flora from around the globe, the grey squirrel has a stronger stomach than the red, which allows it to eat forest food before it is ripe, thereby depriving the red squirrel of much of its food supply. The grey squirrel also carries a disease that is fatal to red squirrels, but to which the grey squirrel itself has developed an immunity.

The muntjac is the oldest known species of deer in the world, having originated in Asia tens of millions of years ago. A large feral population now exists in England, which is thought to have derived from escapees from Woburn Abbey deer park and Whipsnade Zoo in Bedfordshire.

The red deer thrives as Britain's largest mammal, whereas the reindeer reigns supreme in northern Europe as far north as the Arctic Circle, which is why Santa Claus lives in Lapland, of course.

STUFF AND NONSENSE

Rudolph who?

According to the 1823 poem 'A Visit from St Nicholas' (later known as 'The Night Before Christmas'), Santa's eight reindeers were Dasher, Dancer, Prancer, Vixen, Comet, Cupid, Donner and Blitzen (the latter two being the German words for thunder and lightning). Reindeer number nine didn't arrive until 'Rudolph the Red-Nosed Reindeer' flew up the US charts to become the 1949 Christmas number one. If you're old enough (or American enough) to care, it was sung by Gene Autry, known for three decades as 'The Singing Cowboy'.

COOL COLLECTIVES

We all know about a pride of lions and a troop of baboons, but here are some less obvious ones that you may or may not have come across:

1. A congregation of alligators
2. A battery of barracuda
3. A bellowing of bullfinches
4. A clowder of cats
5. A coalition of cheetahs
6. A colony of chinchilla
7. A quiver of cobras
8. A lap of cod
9. A siege of cranes
10. A pace of donkeys
11. A gang of elk
12. A business of flies
13. A tower of giraffes
14. An implausibility of gnus
15. A flamboyance of flamingos
16. A leap of jaguars

17. A smack of jellyfish
18. A mob of kangaroos
19. A lounge of lizards
20. A bite of midges
21. A watch of nightingales
22. A parliament of owls
23. A pomp of Pekingese
24. A bouquet of pheasants
25. A grumble of pugs
26. A rhumba of rattlesnakes
27. An unkindness of ravens
28. A run of salmon
29. A shiver of sharks
30. An audience of squid
31. A murmuration of starlings
32. A fever of stingrays
33. A gulp of swallows
34. A candle of tapirs
35. A mutation of thrush
36. An ambush of tigers
37. A hover of trout
38. A posse of turkeys
39. A blessing of unicorns
40. A venue of vultures
41. A knob of waterfowl
42. A wisdom of wombats
43. A descent of woodpeckers
44. A zeal of zebras

STUFF THAT GROWS

Animals and humans could not survive on planet earth without the many plants and trees that provide everything from oxygen to food. From the rainforest to the desert, different plants and trees find their own ways of surviving and it's only fair that we should stop sometimes to appreciate them.

The red speckled *Rafflesia arnoldii* has the largest flower on earth and is mainly found in Indonesia and Malaysia, where it grows to a diameter of one whole metre (3 ft). It only blossoms for a few days each year and in full bloom it can stink like rotting meat, which attracts pollinating insects in their droves.

The **baobab** tree of Africa and Australia is often called the bottle tree, because it looks like a tall bottle with a bit of foliage sticking out the top. It also resembles a chimney sweep's brush. It is capable of storing so much water that it can live for 5,000 years. The older it gets, the hollower it becomes and it can grow so wide that there is one in South Africa with a drinks bar inside the trunk that can comfortably hold 15 people.

The umbrella-shaped **dragon's blood tree** that grows on the Socotra archipelago off the horn of Africa oozes a red sap which the ancients took for dragon's blood, and which is still used today in medicine, dye, varnish and incense.

Many spectacular varieties of **protea**, or sugarbush, flourish on shrubland known as fynbos in the Western Cape of South Africa. The king protea is the national flower of South Africa and 'the Proteas' is the nickname of the country's national cricket team.

The **Venus flytrap** is a carnivorous plant native to the Carolinas of North America. It will snap its jaws shut if contact is made by an insect or spider on two or more of its hairs within 20 seconds, thereby ensuring that it doesn't waste energy snapping at something that touched it briefly before flying off again.

The mimosa pudica (Latin for 'shy mimosa') is a tropical weed in South and Central America that proves that plants have feelings, since its leaves immediately fold inwards whenever they are touched or shaken. They will remain drooped for a few minutes and only reopen when they think the coast is clear to do so.

A giant sequoia in California called General Sherman is the world's biggest living single-stem tree at 84 metres (275 ft) high and weighing about 1.9 million kg (2,095 tons). It was named by a naturalist who had served in the Indiana Cavalry under General Sherman in the American Civil War.

The beautiful umbrella thorn acacia tree that is the classic image of the Masai Mara in Kenya has a dark secret. It murders animals. When it realises its leaves are being eaten by some grazing animal or other, it releases a gas cloud that warns the next trees in line to produce more tannins in order to make their leaves temporarily toxic. Giraffes have wised up to this and only eat from a single tree before moving on, but some antelopes still get poisoned.

The Victoria amazonica is a giant water lily that grows 3 metres (10 ft) across and has upturned edges that prevent overlapping with its neighbours. They will support a weight of 45 kg (100 pounds), which is about the weight of a child. If you don't believe me, go to Kew Gardens in London and throw your offspring onto one and see what happens.

WHAT HAPPENED EVEN BEFORE HISTORY

INTRODUCTION

It is generally accepted by clever people that the earth was formed about 4.6 billion years ago and that nothing much happened for about 4 billion years after that. Moving swiftly along, then, let's look at the last 600 million years or so, when stuff did actually happen. Earth scientists refer to the last 570 million years as the Phanerozoic aeon (and the previous four billion years as the Precambrian supereon, but who cares, because nothing happened) and then they break the current aeon down into three geological time periods, known as the Paleozoic, Mesozoic and Cenozoic eras. Put into plainer English, that's Greek for 'ancient life', 'middle life' and 'new life', so let's have a look at the three lives of earth.

GETTING STARTED

The Paleozoic era ran from about 542 million years ago to about 250 million years ago. It started when organisms with more than one cell started to organise themselves into three-dimensional structures, which subsequently evolved over millions of years into primitive plants, insects and animals. If you want to know how that can even happen, don't ask me. It's ridiculous, that's all I know.

Then, for reasons which nobody really understands, especially not me, there was a mass extinction, called the Permian–Triassic extinction event. This wiped out 95 per cent of marine species, and a lot of plants and animals besides, before any of them had really had a chance to get going. Luckily enough for us, though, just about enough living things survived to have another go at life on earth.

THE AGE OF THE DINOSAUR

The Mesozoic era ran from about 250 million years ago to about 65 million years ago and was really quite exciting by all accounts. It was split into three periods, the Triassic, the Jurassic and the Cretaceous. We've all at least heard of the Jurassic period for the same reason that we've heard of Indiana Jones and E.T.

Triassic period (250–200 million years ago)

This was meant to be a period of recovery following the mass extinction that preceded it, but the planet remained volatile for a long time. The climate was moving from hot and dry to humid, and the earth was in the very early stages of bursting itself apart from a single landmass into the beginnings of the continents that we recognise today, with more and more of the planet being given over to water. The future east coast of the USA and the future Morocco started to bid farewell to one another, a sign of the many tectonic shifts to come, and early dinosaurs did their best to keep their feet on a moving planet.

Jurassic period (200–145 million years ago)

Also known as the Age of the Ruling Reptiles, this is when dinosaurs established themselves as the dominant force on earth. They were helped by a climate change that delivered the lush rainforests they were able to gorge themselves on, and that is how the really huge ones grew up to be really huge. There was so much to eat that birds, lizards and crocodiles also hurried themselves along the evolutionary scale to ensure they got their fair share of it.

Cretaceous period (145–65 million years ago)

This period was lovely and warm, with no polar ice caps and very high sea levels. The south of England was underwater (which is why the white cliffs of Dover contain billions of fossils from back then), the Atlantic Ocean stretched to fill the ever-widening gap between the future Americas on one side and the future Europe and Africa on the other, and the Indian Ocean was formed. The island of future India bucked the trend to break away by moving up towards the rest of future Asia.

Lush vegetation encouraged vegetarian dinosaurs to eat more and more, so they got bigger and bigger, but the bigger the vegetarian dinosaurs became, the bigger their carnivorous predators became. Evolution had never been easier and life had never felt so good. Until tragedy struck, that is, with another mass extinction.

The end of the dinosaurs

Because the Mesozoic era was brought to its knees only 65 million years ago, earth scientists are prepared to have a guess about what caused it, one theory being that a meteor smashed into what we now know as the Gulf of Mexico (and it's certainly the right shape to have been created by a meteor). Whether a meteor hit there or somewhere else, we do know that something drastic happened to cause huge tectonic shifts, widespread volcanic activity, tsunamis, acid rain and lethal gases rising up from below the earth's surface. The poor dinosaurs never stood a chance. The next time you find yourself worrying about something silly, remember that the next meteor might be along any minute. That's how fragile life on earth is.

They had their day, though, the dinosaurs, ruling the planet for 165 million years (compared to the paltry 200,000 or so years that *Homo sapiens* has had so far). Let us pay homage to a few of our long-lost prehistoric friends, some of whom could barely have brought themselves to dream that they would one day star in their own Steven Spielberg movie.

Name: *Argentinosaurus*
Size: 21 metres (70 ft) tall, 35 metres (115 ft) long
Weight: 80 tons
Where it roamed: Wherever it damn well pleased (but mostly in South America)
Bio: Thriving all the way to the end of the Cretaceous period, this was the heaviest and longest animal ever to roam the earth. The word 'monster' was created for this guy and the earth shook every time it took a step. It was a vegetarian so you had nothing to fear from it unless you got in the way between it and a lush rainforest.
Surprising fact: In spite of its size, a female *Argentinosaurus* laid eggs that were only the size of a rugby ball, so it took 40 years for their babies to become fully grown.

Name: *Giganotosaurus*
Size: 5 metres (16 ft) tall, 15 metres (49 ft) long
Weight: 10 tons
Where it roamed: South America
Bio: The largest of the carnivorous dinosaurs on land, it was so aggressive that it hunted down the *Argentinosaurus*, a prey that was four times taller and eight times heavier than itself. The *Giganotosaurus* had speed on its side, though, and a snappy jaw to die for. Even so, it must have hunted in packs to bring down something as big as an *Argentinosaurus*.
Surprising fact: The *Giganotosaurus* only had a brain the size of a banana, which is probably why it was daft enough to hunt the *Argentinosaurus*.

STUFF AND NONSENSE

Who's the king?

It used to be thought that the *Tyrannosaurus rex* was the largest carnivorous dinosaur, but only because the *Giganotosaurus* wasn't discovered until the late twentieth century. The *Giganotosaurus* of South America was faster as well as bigger, but the *Tyrannosaurus rex* of North America and Mongolia had a bigger brain and was probably the smarter of the two. The T. Rex certainly had more musical talent, being the only one of the two to manage 11 consecutive top-ten singles in the British pop charts.

Name: *Spinosaurus*
Size: 6 metres (20 ft) tall, 15 metres (49 ft) long
Weight: 20 tons
Where it roamed: North Africa
Bio: The largest semi-aquatic carnivorous dinosaur, it was known to hunt on land and in the sea. Imagine a giant crocodile's head and tail with a huge camel in the middle. Just don't call it a big humpbacked lizard to its face in the (admittedly unlikely) event of it making a reappearance.
Surprising fact: In 2001, director Joe Johnston gave the *Spinosaurus* top billing in *Jurassic Park III*, replacing *Tyrannosaurus rex*, the ageing dinosaur that had shot to fame as Steven Spielberg's muse in the first two films.

STUFF AND NONSENSE

'Would Sir like some cranberry sauce with his *Velociraptor*?'

The *Velociraptor* might sound like a dreadful beast, but it was in fact a very small dinosaur. Only the size of a small turkey, it probably came within 75 million years of being the meat of choice for our Christmas and Thanksgiving dinners.

Name: *Pterodactylus antiquus*
Size: 1-metre (3.5-ft) wingspan
Where it roamed: The shores of Europe, South Africa, North America
and Australia
Bio: Everyone's favourite winged reptile, and therefore not really a dinosaur
as such, the *Pterodactylus antiquus* (colloquially known as the Pterodactyl)
was so called – in Greek – because it had 'winged fingers'. In fact, two of
its fingers (one on each hand) were so long that they stretched out towards
the ends of its wings. Pterodactyls preyed on large insects, fish and small
mammals, so they wouldn't have been as terrifying as Hollywood would
have us believe.
Surprising fact: The Pterodactyl was a bit of a runt compared to the
Pteranodon, a similar but much larger winged reptile with a 6-metre
(20-ft) wingspan, so the *Pteranodon* would have been the more likely of
the two to reduce the membership of the Ramblers' Association.

Name: *Stegosaurus*
Size: 4 metres (13 ft) tall, 9 metres (30 ft) long
Weight: 3 tons
Where it roamed: North America, Europe
Bio: One of the so-called 'armoured dinosaurs'. The armour was evolved
more for purposes of defence than attack, although you probably didn't
want to get whacked by its long spiked tail. With stocky limbs and a
huge plated back, it probably resembled a giant rhinoceros on a bad-
hair day.

Surprising fact: The US state of Colorado lists the *Stegosaurus* as its state dinosaur, being one of seven US states to have appointed one. The federal district of Washington, D.C. has also appointed one, after finding the only known trace of a *Creosaurus potens* during excavations to build a new sewer line in 1898. It promptly dubbed the dinosaur *Capitalsaurus*.

THE AGE OF THE MAMMAL

The Cenozoic era that we are living in now has been running for the last 65 million years already. Not quite all species had been wiped out by the mass extinction at the end of the Mesozoic era (just have a look at a crocodile if you have cause to doubt that), but most were. When the earth did finally start to recover during the Cenozoic era, it was a fresh opportunity for the remaining life forms to evolve into new species of plants, animals and birds, but nothing would ever again grow as large as the largest dinosaurs, because the climatic and environmental conditions would never again be right for that to happen. It would, instead, become the age of the mammal, including (eventually) the human being.

Earth scientists have divided the present Cenozoic era into three periods:

Paleogene	65 million to 23 million years ago
Neogene	23 million to 2.6 million years ago
Quaternary	2.6 million years ago to present day

Paleogene period

It took the first ten million years of this period for the earth to bounce back to health after its second mass extinction, but it eventually did so in spectacular fashion, with an increasingly warm and humid climate and a jungle environment that spread as far as both poles.

Taking shape

At the start of the Paleogene period, continents carried on drifting apart and oceans continued to fill the gaps until the basic geography of the world started to look as it does to us now, although India was still an island, the Americas were still separated by the Strait of Panama, and the Tethys Sea continued to separate Africa and the Middle East.

As the period wore on, massive glacial activity put further pressure on the earth's tectonic plates, causing the mountain ranges we know today to rise up. The Rocky Mountains in North America were shaped by glacial erosion, the Alps in Europe rose up when the African continent decided to move north, and the Himalayas of Asia were largely formed when the island of India finally joined itself onto the continent of Asia.

Small is beautiful

As far as the animal kingdom was concerned at the start of the Paleogene period, small mammals, birds, reptiles and amphibians spread happily across a world devoid of larger predators (in the jungle, small is beautiful, because larger animals bump into trees and find it generally difficult to get around), and this period of relative stability led to widespread evolution and diversification. Parrots, woodpeckers, rabbits, hares and armadillos are among the modern-day species to make their first appearance.

Flightless birds grew larger than any other creature on earth and found themselves at the top of the food chain, pretty much ruling the world for a while. Plant life also thrived and diversified without the dinosaurs to munch their way through it as if there were no tomorrow. In the absence of the giant aquatic dinosaurs that had once ruled the seas, even marine life was small. Whales, sea cows and sharks were miniature versions of their present-day selves.

Growing room

There then followed a cooling period and a return to seasonal weather. This shrank the jungles, creating savannahs and grasses in their place and allowing mammals to do a bit of growing again out in the open. On land, this culminated in the *Paraceratherium*, a hornless rhinoceros that remains one of the largest terrestrial mammals to have ever existed. In the air, it led to the *Pelagornis sandersi*, a bird with twice the wingspan of the largest albatross. In the sea, whales began to grow exponentially and were on their way to becoming the giants that we know and love today.

Neogene period

As jungles and forests continued to shrink, the planet revealed itself to be increasingly mountainous and arid, but good grazing land still filled the valleys and plains. An abundance of grasses and evergreen trees led to the evolution of more and more grazers and sky predators. Among those to join the feast were mammoths, elephants, giraffes, rhinoceroses, marsupials, horses, antelopes, zebras, tapirs, eagles and many different species of apes. Lions, hyenas, bears and sabre-toothed tigers were so delighted to see the grazers that they evolved just so they could eat them.

Onwards and upwards

It is fairly common knowledge that the *Homo* (man) and *Pan* (chimpanzee) genera share a common ancestor. It is difficult to be certain about the exact time we went our separate ways, but it was probably sometime between 13 million and 4 million years ago, probably the result of some spat at a tea party. On the non-chimpanzee side of things, *Australopithecus* then emerged in eastern Africa and eventually evolved about two million years ago into *Homo habilis*, or 'handy man'. If you had a leaky cave, *Homo habilis* was the man to fix it (and, quite ironically, it was paleoanthropologist Mary Leakey who discovered the first trace of *Homo habilis* in Tanzania in 1955).

It took a little while longer (until about 1.9 million years ago) for *Homo erectus* to start looking a bit less ape-like, and longer still (until about 200,000 years ago) for *Homo sapiens* to start thinking on its own two feet.

But life wouldn't always be so easy for the proliferating fauna and flora of the Neogene period, because cold weather was on its way. And when I say cold, I mean cold. The sort of glacial cold you get when you are entering an ice age, and which does funny things to the landscape of a planet. Narrow stretches of water, for example, like the English Channel and the Bering Strait (between Siberia and Alaska), would soon freeze over to become land bridges.

STUFF AND NONSENSE

Great American Interchange

When volcanic activity caused much land to rise out of the sea towards the end of the Neogene period, the Strait of Panama filled itself in and became the Isthmus of Panama. The mammals of the previously separate continents of North America and South America looked at this new land bridge and saw an opportunity to travel like never before. Imagine the look on an armadillo's face as it ambled up to California and saw a bear or a raccoon heading past in the opposite direction.

Quaternary period (the one we're in now)

When this period kicked off 2.6 million years ago, it was the beginning of an ice age that continues to this day. That's right, we're living in an ice age, which we can tell by looking at the amount of ice in the Arctic and Antarctic regions and on Greenland. Luckily for us, though, most of the planet isn't covered in these ice sheets, which is how we can tell we're living in an interglacial period. As you might expect, this is much warmer than living in one of the glacial periods that continue to come and go, sooner or later. Earth scientists split the current Quaternary period into two epochs:

Pleistocene   2.6 million years ago to 12,000 years ago
Holocene   12,000 years ago to the present time

Pleistocene epoch

The ice sheets this epoch started with covered much of the planet, including a stretch across North America from future Seattle to future New York. Towards the end of the epoch, the Great Lakes were formed when the glaciers finally receded, resulting in a proliferation of freshwater fish and allowing forests to once more overrun the land. The shape of the world's continents, seas and lakes were settling into pretty much what they are today.

Ice-age extinctions

It is thought that the current ice age peaked (i.e. was at its coldest) about 195,000 years ago, when the Arctic ice cap reached down to the equator, freezing many species to death in the process. Sub-equatorial Africa was about the only place on earth that remained habitable, which is why it has sufficient diversity in its wildlife to remain the world's main safari destination to this day, and why it is the area in which we find the earliest fossil records of modern humans. There were other ice-age extinctions as well, though, and here are just some of the species that did not survive one or other of them:

Woolly mammoth: the most studied of all prehistoric creatures on account of frozen carcasses found in Siberia and Alaska. Its closest extant relative is the Asian elephant, but it was probably the size of the bigger African elephant, with longer tusks.

Sabre-toothed tiger (officially known as *Smilodon*): roamed North and South America. The largest fossil found to date confirms teeth that were 28 centimetres (11 inches) long.

Teratornis: roamed the skies of North America. Similar to, but bigger than, the giant condor, it had a wingspan up to 4 metres (12 ft).

Giant beaver (*Castoroides*): at 2.5 metres (8 ft) long, this was the largest rodent of its time, found in North America.

Irish elk: at 2 metres (7 ft) tall, with antlers 4 metres (12 ft) wide, it was one of the largest ever deer, but it wasn't an elk. It wasn't just Irish either, because it has also been found in Europe, Asia and North Africa.

Holocene epoch

Finally, we arrive in our own time: the Holocene epoch of the Quaternary period of the Cenozoic era. Our own little epoch has only been on the go for about 12,000 years, since the glaciers last retreated and the forests last re-established themselves, so it is just a baby in geological speak.

At the start of our epoch the 'great melt' increased sea levels around the globe by an average of 90 metres (295 ft). To put that sea change into context, environmentalists are currently worried about the possibility of global warming increasing sea levels by up to a metre (3.28 ft). The British Isles were established in their current form as the Irish Sea deglaciated and the English Channel flooded. Since then, notwithstanding current concerns about human impact, we have enjoyed a relatively stable climate and environment. We did have a bit of global warming from the tenth to the thirteenth centuries (the Medieval Warm Period) and a Little Ice Age from the fourteenth to the nineteenth centuries, but they were nothing to worry about really.

Although we are young as epochs ago, quite a lot has happened during our infancy, which has mostly consisted of the so-called Stone Age.

Stone Age

Although *Homo erectus* had been having a bit of a bash with stone for about three million years already, particularly in the Rift Valley of Africa, it was *Homo sapiens*, as you might expect, who started to put stone to a greater variety of uses. In order to keep track of the prolific output of our Stone Age ancestors, in fact, archaeologists divide the so-called Stone Age into three periods: Paleolithic, Mesolithic and Neolithic (after the Greek for 'old stone', 'middle stone' and 'new stone').

Notwithstanding its reputation with stone at the time, though, *Homo sapiens* also made extensive use of wood, bone, shell and antler. In other words, our ancestors used whatever they could get their hands on for as many purposes as they could, including the following ones:

1. Fighting: to defend themselves against wild animals and unfriendly tribes.
2. Hunting: to spear everything from fish to mammoths.
3. Housing: to provide shelter in the absence of a decent available cave in the area.
4. Preparing food: from harvesting vegetables to cutting into dead animals, in particular to get at the much-prized liver, kidneys and brains (which was an offal thing to do, I know).
5. Drawing: to make their caves nice and maybe even one day get a much-coveted World Heritage Site award.
6. Building monuments: to worship their primitive gods, the most famous of the monuments being Stonehenge.
7. Making clothing and jewellery: to cut up animal hides for clothing and string shells together to make primitive necklaces and the like.
8. Making music: mostly percussion, I should think, but 'rock music' had to start somewhere.
9. Digging: to sow seeds (agriculture started to be adopted towards the end of the Stone Age) and, in some cultures, to bury their dead.

The end of prehistory

By the time *Homo sapiens* started to get really clever, which was about 5,000 years ago, it was time to stop being prehistoric and get civilised. Religion, agriculture, writing, metal tools and weaponry were about to burst forth around the world in the so-called Bronze Age, the earliest recognised period of civilised history and where we will, therefore, pick up the story in the next chapter. Prehistory was about to become a thing of the past, and the rest, as they say, is history.

WHAT HAPPENED DURING HISTORY

INTRODUCTION

There have been over 5,000 years of history already and we're going to have to race through it here, so hold on to your hats as we cover some seriously major periods and events at breakneck speed. In order to keep things vaguely chronological, I've split it into three main eras:

Long time ago (Ancient)	3600 BCE–500 CE
The middle bit (Medieval)	500 CE–1500 CE
A bit more up to date (Modern)	1500 CE–present

Let's have a quick word about this BCE and CE thing before we start. We used to always say BC (before Christ) and AD (Anno Domini), but the world's historians are trying to standardise their dating conventions a bit, which has the added benefit of being a bit more inclusive from a faith point of view. So now we can use Before Common Era (BCE) and Common Era (CE) instead, which is what I have done in this book, because I'm a modern kind of a guy. No conversions will be necessary, because BCE equates exactly with BC and CE equates exactly with AD.

LONG-TIME-AGO HISTORY, 3600 BCE–500 CE

This era pretty much started when people started to live together in purpose-built cities in major river valleys or coastal areas around the world, heralding the start of vast unrelated civilisations around the globe. These civilisations quickly became adept at irrigating the land from the rivers and seas they lived beside, which in turn allowed them to grow their own food along with fodder for their livestock. They learned to smelt, cast and forge metals in order to produce bronze weaponry, tools and decorative objects, and the progress they made in this respect led historians to dub this period of history the Bronze Age from around 3000 BCE onwards (more exact dates depended on which civilisation you belonged to). Once these same civilisations progressed to working with more durable iron, from about 1000 BCE onwards, the historians once again put their imagination to the test and came up with Iron Age to describe the next 1,500 years or so.

Once people started to live together in large numbers within these early civilisations, they also started to feel the need for common beliefs, resulting in as many religions as there were civilisations. Once they started to develop a sense of their own history, they felt the urge to record it for posterity, initially by passing it on through the spoken word and then in written form.

Most of these civilisations collapsed sooner or later after becoming too big for their boots. Some were unable to content themselves with what they had or couldn't resist the urge to conquer elsewhere; others felt the need to convert other religions to their own set of beliefs. They all had their day, though, each one magnificent in its own way. Let us have a look at a few of the main ones:

The empires of Mesopotamia (3600 BCE–1258 CE)

These were situated in the Middle East between the Euphrates and Tigris rivers (present-day Iraq, Syria and Kuwait), which is why the Ancient Greeks called the region Mesopotamia ('between two rivers'). An oasis somewhere within the region is believed by many to be the site of the Garden of Eden, and it was certainly the first part of the world to play host to civilised empires, including those of the Sumerians, Assyrians and Babylonians. It was in this area that cuneiform, one of the earliest writing systems (using wedge-shaped marks on clay tablets), was developed.

Archaeologists have unearthed a vast amount of evidence that people lived well in impressive cities like Ur and Babylon, notwithstanding a lot of irritating invasions by the likes of the Hittites, Greeks, Romans, Persians and Muslims all the way through to the Middle Ages. The Mongols finally laid waste to the region in 1258 when they destroyed what was left of the ancient irrigation system.

Indus Valley Civilisation (3300 BCE–1300 BCE)

The planned cities of this vast Bronze Age civilisation flourished along the fertile valleys of the Indus river in parts of modern-day Afghanistan, Pakistan, China and India. Important excavations have taken place at a site near the village of Harappa in what is now Pakistan, having been unearthed by the British during construction of the East Indian Railway Company Line between Karachi and Lahore in 1856. They realised its archaeological importance, but not before they had used a fair bit of it as ballast in the construction of the railway. Later excavations in the 1920s revealed a fortified city with enough clay-sculpted houses for a population of over 20,000.

Ancient Egypt (3200 BCE–641 CE)

Built along the life-supporting River Nile, developments in technology, art and architecture enabled the building of the pyramid tombs to provide for the afterlife of the all-powerful pharaohs. This was nice for the pharaohs, of course, but not so nice for the many builders who collapsed and died in the searing heat.

The hieroglyphic records of Ancient Egypt tell us much about its history, but they remained indecipherable until after a French soldier unearthed the Rosetta Stone in 1799 during the Napoleonic expedition to Egypt. The stone provided the key because it contained translations of the hieroglyphs on it in two other languages, Demotic and Ancient Greek, both of which were understood by scholars.

Following the death of the last great pharaoh Ramesses III in 1155 BCE, Egypt started to split up, leaving itself vulnerable to one conquering invader after another. The Kushites, Assyrians, Persians, Greeks, Romans and Muslims all took their turn. When the Romans took their turn in the first century BCE, they were probably surprised to find that the reigning queen (Cleopatra) was a Greek. They were probably even more surprised by the level of Cleopatra's hospitality as she proceeded to provide both Julius Caesar and Mark Antony with offspring.

The culture and traditions of Ancient Egypt were not overly discouraged by its successive conquerors until the Muslims finally quashed them following their victory at the Siege of Alexandria in 641 CE.

Ancient China (1766 BCE–220 CE)

The Yellow River supported many Bronze and Iron Age settlements and several warring kingdoms until China got its act together and became the most advanced civilisation in the world for a long time to come.

The man to unite the kingdoms was First Emperor Qin (pronounced 'chin', hence China) in 221 BCE. His achievements, in addition to conquering the rest of China, included combining various existing defensive walls to create the Great Wall of China, which is over 21,000 km (13,000 miles) long, to keep out invading Huns and other nomadic invaders from the north, and the creation of his tomb at Xi'an containing a vast terracotta army to guard his body in the afterlife.

Terracotta Army

It took 700,000 workers 38 years to build First Emperor Qin's tomb, complete with 8,000 brightly painted life-size foot soldiers and officers, each one with different facial features, as well as hundreds of horses and 130 grand chariots. Many treasures were buried along with the emperor's body when the time came, and the tomb was only rediscovered after some 2,000 years by some farmers digging a well in 1974.

Inventors and innovators

The Ancient Chinese were great inventors and innovators, although it sometimes took centuries for the rest of the world to reap the benefits because the Chinese were geographically remote and perfectly self-sufficient without contacting the wider world. Here are just some of the things they came up with way ahead of everyone else:

1. Paper and printing: including the first paper money.
2. Silk: not just for clothing, but also for fishing lines, musical strings, bow strings and luxury paper.
3. Cast iron: which they moulded into tools and weapons.
4. Gunpowder: made their cast-iron weapons a bit more effective (and meant they no longer had to shout Bang! when they kicked the back of the cannon).
5. Wheelbarrow: which they called the 'wooden ox'.
6. Bristle toothbrush: for getting those pesky bits of rice out of the back cavities.
7. Acupuncture: the insertion of needles to stimulate nerves is still popular to this day to restore our Qi and treat everything from back pain to insomnia.
8. Magnetic compass: useful for mapping the stars (they didn't really need it to get around China, because everyone knew that north was over the wall, east was turn right at the wall, and so on).
9. Ships with rudders: they might not look it now, but Chinese junks were once the most advanced ships in the world.
10. Alcoholic beverage: the fermentation of fruit, rice and honey (which sounds like a perfectly balanced diet to me).
11. Luxury goods: from silk paintings to black laquerwork and not forgetting the ever-popular Ming vase.

12. Nail polish: made from a mixture of egg whites, beeswax, gelatin, gum Arabic and dyes (which I mention in case you want to have a go at making your own).

13. Chopsticks: we have had over 2,000 years to get the hang of these, and I'm still useless with them.

14. Clockwork: to make sure all their other inventions arrived on time.

Confucius (551–479 BCE)

A great and respected thinker, teacher, philosopher and politician who had a lasting influence on Chinese society and beyond, many of his ancient pearls of wisdom, like the three that follow, hold good today:

> *Our greatest glory is not in never falling,*
> *but in getting up every time we do.*

> *Real knowledge is to know the extent of one's ignorance.*

> *I hear and I forget. I see and I remember. I do and I understand.*

Ancient Greece (800 BCE–600 CE)

For the first few centuries of its existence Greece was divided into a large number of warring city-states, the two main ones being Athens and Sparta, but this didn't stop them from making the sort of progress that continues to influence the world we live in today. Here are just a few of the things they gave to the world:

1. Democracy: allowed every adult male citizen the right to vote in every major public decision.
2. Law and order: devised by the legislator Draco, who made extensive use of the death penalty (which you might rightly consider a bit 'draconian'), and later softened by the politician Solon.
3. Marathon running: the first such run was undertaken by Pheidippides in 490 BCE when he ran the 40 km (25 miles) from Marathon to Athens to announce an important victory over the Persians, and then promptly died of exhaustion.
4. Olympic Games: all wars were halted once every four years to allow safe passage for all athletes to and from Olympia.
5. Proper history: Herodotus was the first to research and verify past events before writing them down.
6. Philosophy: Socrates, Plato and Aristotle are considered to be the fathers of Western philosophy (which is itself the Greek word for 'love of wisdom').
7. Drama: tragedy, comedy and satire were the order of the day and show no signs of abating thousands of years later.
8. Greek words, which we still use to this day within the English language, like photograph, astronomy, phobia, micro, phenomenon and alphabet (from the first two letters of the Greek alphabet).

Alexander the Great

Thanks to Alexander the Great's military prowess in the fourth century BCE, Greece was finally unified and was able to stretch its borders all the way to Central Asia in the east and the Mediterranean in the west. Born in Macedonia and educated by Aristotle, Alexander was only 20 when he became king and by the time he died in Babylon at the tender age of 32 the area he had conquered included modern-day Turkey, Syria, Egypt, Iran, Iraq, Pakistan and India. He imposed Greek culture and philosophy wherever he went and conquered peoples everywhere were heard to say, 'We might have been invaded by Alexander the Great, but you have to be philosophical about these things.'

Ancient Rome (753 BCE–476 CE)

Having been established on its legendary seven hills in 753 BCE, Ancient Rome was ruled initially by some fairly unpleasant kings, the last of whom was overthrown in 510 BCE so that a republic of senators could have a go. Things went a bit better then, as the patricians were pretty good at running a senate and even the plebeians were allowed to have a say.

Various military excursions extended Roman influence, notwithstanding some tough campaigns against pesky Celtic tribes, Carthaginians (including a surprise attack by Hannibal after he marched some elephants across the Alps) and the escaped gladiator Spartacus. Their well-drilled armies eventually conquered most of Europe, North Africa and the Middle East, in spite of internal wrangling amongst their all-conquering generals, some dodgy triumvirates and some even dodgier emperors, notably the following:

1. Julius Caesar: declared himself dictator for life but then forgot to beware the Ides of March.

2. Mark Antony: when it came to Cleopatra, he just couldn't keep his snake in his trousers and they both ended up having to commit suicide after military defeat.

3. Octavian/Augustus: Rome's first, and arguably finest, emperor. Once he had hunted down Great-Uncle Julius's assassins, he ruled strongly for over 40 years.

4. Caligula: thought he was either a god or the much-discussed Messiah of the Jews, and appointed his horse Incitatus as a priest.

5. Nero: had his own mother murdered and allegedly fiddled with his lyre while Rome burned.

6. Hadrian: there was no one better at building walls but he had his lover Antinous declared a god, which is right up there with making your horse a priest.

7. Constantine the Great: turned Christian and moved his capital to Byzantium, which he modestly renamed Constantinople (now Istanbul). He left Rome at the mercy of the Visigoths, who promptly sacked it, and that was the end of Ancient Rome.

While all this conquering and in-fighting and general madness was going on, though, the Romans still managed to bring improvements to the living standards of those they conquered. So, what exactly did the Romans do for us and the other peoples they subjugated?

1. Introduced the Julian calendar, which was the first to have 12 months, 365 days and leap years.

2. Gave us forenames and surnames (Greeks had generally stuck with one).
3. Conferred much-prized Roman citizenship on a lot of their new subjects, including freed slaves.
4. Allowed women to own property and become rich in their own right.
5. Shared their advanced architecture, engineering and building prowess, giving us straight roads, aqueducts, viaducts, baths and 50,000-seater stadiums like the Colosseum.
6. Taught us Latin, much of which we still use to this day, like vice versa, ad hoc, quid pro quo, post mortem, mea culpa (Latin for 'my bad') and carpe diem.
7. Showed us how to count in tens, and gave us Roman numerals for our clock faces.

Celtic tribes

Celtic tribes spanned central Europe from around 600 BCE, and by 275 BCE they dominated much of Europe, having built well-defended hill forts everywhere from Scotland in the north to Turkey in the south, from Spain in the south-west to the Balkan lands of eastern Europe. They were fierce warriors but also skilled metalworkers, and their art was instantly recognisable by their trademark swirling patterns. They shared common pagan beliefs (their religious leaders being the Druids) as well as related languages, including Scottish Gaelic, Welsh, Irish and Breton, but they never really joined up in any cohesive or disciplined fashion. They often preferred to go into battle naked as a sign of personal bravery and they were a constant thorn in the side of the Romans.

Queen Boudicca (or Boadicea)

Perhaps the most famous Celtic warrior of them all, Boudicca rebelled against Roman invasion in 60 CE in a way that many male warrior leaders had lacked the bottle to do themselves. Having been flogged and having seen her daughters raped by the Romans, she led her Iceni tribe to many victories and destroyed several important Roman cities.

Seven Wonders of the Ancient World

Before we leave ancient history behind and spring forward into the Middle Ages, let us pay homage to the seven most wondrous of its many wonders:

1. Great Pyramid at Giza (2500 BCE): The first of the Seven Wonders to be built and the only one to still stand, it was the tallest building in the world for nearly 4,000 years until Lincoln Cathedral was built in England in 1300 CE.
2. Hanging Gardens of Babylon (c550 BCE): Supposedly built by King Nebuchadnezzar II for his queen, although no historical remains have ever been found.
3. Statue of Zeus (435 BCE): A 13-metre (43-ft) wooden statue covered in ivory and gold built inside a temple in Olympia in southern Greece.
4. Mausoleum at Halicarnassus (350 BCE): A quite fantastic white-marble tomb for Mausolus, the ruler of Caria in modern-day Turkey. It stood until 1522 CE when it was destroyed by earthquakes.

5. Temple of Artemis (323 BCE): Built in the holy city of Ephesus in modern-day Turkey, this was the largest Greek temple ever built.
6. Lighthouse (or Pharos) of Alexandria (247 BCE): One of the tallest man-made buildings in the world at the time, this huge lighthouse made Alexandria the only safe harbour in the Mediterranean. Rocked by earthquakes, it finally toppled into the sea in the fifteenth century.
7. Colossus of Rhodes (280 BCE): a huge bronze-and-iron statue built in Rhodes harbour by the Greeks to thank the sun god Helios for delivering them from a terrible siege. It took 12 years to build, fell down after 60 years and lay toppled for a further 800 years.

THE MIDDLE BIT OF HISTORY, 500–1500 CE

Once the Romans finally went back to Rome to be just Romans again, they took their civilisation with them and European tribes everywhere went straight back to fighting each other, thereby making it easy for the Vikings to sneak up and slaughter them one by one.

Britain would have to wait until the Norman conquest of 1066 to finally see some order and decorum restored, and it would take until the Renaissance of the fourteenth century for thinkers, writers and artists to finally turn back to the cultures of Ancient Greece and Rome, thereby allowing Europeans to finish the Middle Ages with a bit of a flourish.

In the absence of any decent government anywhere for hundreds of years, the Catholic Church saw a gap in the market and turned itself into the richest and most powerful institution in Europe, but even that was dwarfed by the rise of Islam in the Middle East, as Muslim armies conquered vast areas and established magnificent cities like Cairo, Baghdad and Damascus.

Elsewhere, Chinese civilisation continued to blossom, the Mayans, Aztecs and Incas of Mesoamerica carried on in blissful ignorance of the horrors to come at the hands of the Spanish, the Mongols under Genghis Khan were being very bad boys indeed, and Hinduism took over from Buddhism as the main religion of India, only to be suppressed by conquering Muslim sultans.

Let's have a look at some of the highlights of the so-called Middle Ages.

Britain starts to take shape

In the fifth century, without any Romans in the way, Angles, Jutes and Saxons sailed across from northern Europe to push indigenous Celtic tribes north and west into Wales, Ireland and Scotland, where they pretty much remain to this day. Those left behind in England became Anglo-Saxons under Germanic or Danish rule, which meant a degree of stability and a lot of new farming methods, but tribal warfare remained a bit of an issue throughout the land.

The golden age of Islam (eighth to thirteenth century CE)

The golden age of Islam began with the founding of the House of Wisdom in Baghdad under the caliphate of Harun al-Rashid in the late eighth century.

Scholars from around the world were invited to the House of Wisdom to share ideas and knowledge, study the humanities, sciences and arts and translate all of the world's classical knowledge into Arabic. By the middle of the ninth century, it housed the largest selection of books in the world.

The knowledge gained during this golden age of learning was put to practical use in the centuries that followed as advances were made in healthcare, education, economics, trade, astronomy, science, mathematics and architecture, but the flourishing society met a horrible end with the Sack of Baghdad in 1258. Invading Mongol forces looted and destroyed mosques, palaces, hospitals and libraries, including the House of Wisdom itself, and estimates of the number of people slaughtered range from 90,000 to a million.

The Vikings (800–1100 CE)

The Vikings of Scandinavia marauded here, there and everywhere in their impressive longboats for around 300 years, commandeering much of coastal Europe and even popping over to America 500 years before Christopher Columbus. Some were vicious pirates, killing, raping, pillaging and burning as they went. Others were genuine explorers looking to find new lands to settle in away from the bitter winters of their homeland.

The ambition of every warrior was to die bravely on the battlefield, because that would secure a ride with the Valkyries, the warrior women who would transport you to Valhalla, where the god Odin himself would welcome you, following which you got to feast every night for eternity. Well worth an axe in the head, I would have thought.

Kings of wherever

It was difficult to keep up with who was king of which bits of the British Isles and elsewhere for a long time. By way of example, we had Alfred the Great ruling from 871 to 899 as King of Wessex while the Danes still ruled northern England; Æthelstan ruling from 924 to 939 as King of Mercia and Wessex, then all of England, then all of Britain; and Cnut ruling from 1016 to 1035 as King of England, Denmark and Norway. Things settled down with the House of Normandy established by William the Conqueror, the first of six dynasties (the others being Plantagenet, Tudor, Stuart, Saxe-Coburg and Gotha, and Windsor) that take us through to the present day.

House of Normandy (1066–1154):

William I the Conqueror (1066–1087)
William II Rufus (1087–1100)
Henry I (1100–1135)
Stephen (1135–1154)

Knights in shining armour (1066–c.1500)

After William the Conqueror won the Battle of Hastings in 1066 in Battle (as opposed to Hastings, which is miles away), those who submitted to his iron rule were at least allowed to appreciate the finer things in life, like manners, chivalry and jolly jousts. When you took off your heavy chainmail after a hard day out fighting for your (French) king, you could munch on a nice leg of deer in a lovely stone castle while listening to the latest hits by The Troubadours and protesting to all the pretty maidens that you couldn't possibly dance in the French way, what with your two left feet. There were some downsides, though, like the high taxes you had to pay according to your entry in the Domesday Book of 1086, and there was always the chance of getting roped into a crusade or two.

It's not as hard to find le mot juste as you might think

The English language pretty much disappeared following the Norman conquest as the victors set about ruling in their own language. William the Conqueror spoke nothing but Norman French at his coronation in Westminster Abbey on Christmas Day, 1066, and soon Norman French was the prevailing language of everything from the law court and its prisons to the markets and kitchens of the common people.

By the time it got difficult to tell who was originally Norman and who was originally Anglo-Saxon, it wasn't really an option for anyone to go back to speaking Olde English because it had pretty much disappeared. Eventually the English would recreate an identity and language of their own, but their new language mostly evolved from pronouncing French really badly and calling it English. To name but one of countless examples, consider the difference between the soft sound of French *justice* and the harsher sound of English justice. In other words, the English did to French *justice* what the Americans later did to the English tomato.

House of Plantagenet (1154–1485):

Henry II (1154–1189)
Richard I the Lionheart
   (1189–1199)
John (1199–1216)
Henry III (1216–1272)
Edward I Longshanks (1272–1307)
Edward II (1307–1327)
Edward III (1327–1377)

Richard II (1377–1399)
Henry IV (1399–1413)
Henry V (1413–1422)
Henry VI (1422–1461)
Edward IV (1461–1483)
Edward V (1483)
Richard III (1483–1485)

Eventful stuff of the Plantagenet era

The Plantagenet kings of England carried on in the pure French tradition and language until the Hundred Years' War with France eventually made that a bit embarrassing. In 1339, therefore, Henry IV became the first English ruler to make a coronation speech in English since before the Norman conquest of 1066, and in 1415 Henry V further broke with tradition by sending his dispatches from Agincourt in English. Here are some other nuggets of information about Plantagenet England:

1170: Henry II had Thomas Becket, Archbishop of Canterbury, murdered in Canterbury Cathedral because he wouldn't do as he was told.

1185: Lincoln Cathedral was destroyed by an earthquake.

1215: King John signed the Magna Carta, which limited the powers of the crown and established the basis of British law.

1346–1353: The Black Death, a bubonic plague that caused skin to turn black, killed a third of the population of England and up to 200 million people worldwide.

1381: The introduction of a poll tax caused the Peasants' Revolt led by Wat Tyler, who was killed for his impudence.

1483: Edward V, aged 12, and his younger brother Prince Richard (aka the Princes in the Tower) were murdered in the Tower of London so that uncle Richard III could be king instead.

1485: Richard III was killed on Bosworth Field in the final significant battle of the Wars of the Roses.

2012: The body of Richard III was rediscovered under a car park in Leicester.

The Crusades (1095–1291)

The capture and plunder of Palestine in 1076 by Muslim Turks led to nine Christian crusades to the Holy Land over the next couple of centuries. The First Crusade led by the Normans led to the recapture of Jerusalem in 1099 after they massacred its Muslim and Jewish inhabitants. Saladin, sultan of Egypt and Syria, recaptured it in 1187, prompting the partially successful Third Crusade which was led in part by Richard the Lionheart of England. There was one unofficial crusade, dubbed the Children's Crusade, in 1212, when tens of thousands of European teenagers got a bit caught up with the whole religious fervour thing and marched off to die of hunger and thirst without ever reaching the Holy Land.

Richard I of England, my foot!

Lionhearted he may have been, but during his ten-year reign of England, Richard I spent less than six months in the country, preferring to spend his time in the south of France when he wasn't away on crusade to the Holy Land. His parents, Henry II and the formidable Eleanor of Aquitaine, were of French Norman descent, his native tongue was French (he barely spoke a word of English), he often said that he would sell England if he could find a buyer, and he left instructions for his heart to be buried in France upon his death.

His absences did lead to his brother, the future King John, getting a bit big for his boots, which in turn led to the barons forcing him to sign the Magna Carta in 1215, so perhaps we at least have the Lionheart (or should that be Cœur de Lion?) to thank for the ongoing basis of the British legal system.

The Hundred Years' War (1337–1453)

The Hundred Years' War was waged over English claims on the French crown and certain French territories, which the French were understandably none too happy about. It lasted for 116 years and five French and five English kings. It was a bit on and off, not least because the Black Death stopped play for about ten years after decimating both armies. It is remembered mostly for the following iconic moments in history:

1346: First major victory goes to Edward III of England at the Battle of Crécy despite being seriously outnumbered, thanks to the prowess of his son the Black Prince and the introduction of the longbow.

1415: Henry V of England attacks once more into the breach and secures a famous victory at Agincourt, despite the English being outnumbered again.

1429: A peasant teenage girl called Jeanne d'Arc (Joan of Arc) shows the boys how it's done by helping French forces to break the English siege of Orléans. She is burned at the stake for her trouble, but it is the turning point of the war in France's favour.

1453: End of the war and overall victory for France, with England only getting Calais and the Channel Islands.

Genghis Khan

In 12 short years between 1215 and 1227, Genghis Khan and his nomadic Mongol horde brought devastation and slaughter on an unprecedented scale to Persia, southern Russia, China, Armenia, northern India and eastern Europe (making the squabbles between England and France look like medieval handbags at dawn). The Mongols fought on horseback and won their battles through a combination of ferocity, great tactical awareness and new technology such as gunpowder in guns and rockets. Genghis Khan's sons and grandsons carried on where he left off and around 30 million people would die at Mongol hands by the time they were finished. It took around 150 years for the Chinese to drive them out, whereupon they established the Ming dynasty and set about creating orderly government, social stability and the fine vases that remain much sought after to this day.

Ottoman empire (1299–1922)

Founded in 1299 by Osman I, leader of the Ottoman Turks, the Ottoman empire went on to become one of the world's great empires, led by a succession of sultans. They ended the Byzantine (Eastern Roman) empire after taking Constantinople (modern-day Istanbul) in 1453, and their eventual control over the eastern Mediterranean and North African regions allowed them to forge a multinational, multilingual civilisation. It reached its peak under the tenth sultan, Suleiman the Magnificent, who reigned from 1520 to 1566 and presided over major advances in art, literature, architecture, education, taxation and law.

The empire eventually suffered a slow decline in the nineteenth century and was extinguished entirely following defeat in the First World War, after which modern-day Turkey was created in its place.

Mayans, Aztecs and Incas (up to sixteenth century)

Although the Mayans of Mesoamerica (which is largely modern-day Central America and southern Mexico) were amongst the earliest of the world's ancient civilisations, dating back to around 2000 BCE, they enjoyed their golden age from around 250 to 900 CE, during which time they excelled in writing, mathematics, art, astronomy and architecture. They were ruled over by various city-states, most notably that of Chichén Itzá.

The Incas also descended from ancient civilisations, primarily along the Andes mountain range in modern-day Peru, north Chile, Ecuador, south-west Bolivia and north-west Argentina. They came together as the single Inca Empire with the founding of the city of Cusco in *c.*1200 CE and went on to build the city of Machu Picchu in the middle of the fifteenth century.

The Aztecs settled in the Valley of Mexico in the thirteenth century CE and built their capital city Teotihuacán near where Mexico City now stands. They mainly flourished from 1440 to 1469 under Montezuma I, who presided over the expansion of the empire and the building of all-important aqueducts to supply fresh water.

The three civilisations had two things in common: the huge temples and human sacrifices they offered up to their gods, and their demise at the start of the sixteenth century at the hands of the Spanish conquistadors, who meted out slaughter and smallpox in equal measure.

BRINGING HISTORY UP TO DATE (1500–PRESENT)

Around the world in 500 years

You might think that the period of the last 500 years isn't exactly up to date, but it is when considered in the overall span of history. At the turn of the sixteenth century, the Americas had just been 'discovered', the Renaissance was in full swing, books could be printed and the Tudors were up and running after Henry VII emerged victorious from the Wars of the Roses and married Elizabeth of York to unite the two houses of York and Lancaster.

Let's have a brief look first at some of the most significant events around the world in so-called modern history, before returning to complete our canter through the royal dynasties of Britain (we still have Tudor, Stuart, Hanover, Saxe-Coburg and Gotha and Windsor to go).

The Renaissance (fourteenth to seventeenth century)

Beginning in Italy in the fourteenth century and soon spreading across Europe, this 'rebirth' of interest in learning and in the arts was inspired to a large extent by greater contact with Muslim and Far East cultures. There was a move away from divinity in all things to humanism and the thoughts and abilities of the individual. Backed by powerful families like the Medici in Florence, and inspired by the universal genius of Leonardo da Vinci, artists like Michelangelo and Botticelli portrayed the human form with greater realism and poets like Dante and Petrarch looked deeper into the human soul.

   In northern Europe the Renaissance was adopted with vigour and led to the Protestant Reformation – a stand against the widespread power and corruption of the Roman Catholic Church. The Catholics rejected all compromise and launched their own Counter-Reformation, spearheaded by the Jesuit order. The entrenched positions of the two religious groups led to bloody war after bloody war, culminating in the Thirty Years' War (1618–1648), which resulted in religious stalemate but greater sovereignty for individual nations across Europe.

The Mughal Empire (sixteenth to nineteenth century)

After Babur, a Muslim Turkish descendant of Genghis Khan, defeated the sultan of Delhi in 1526, his territory became known as the Mughal (a variation of Mongol) Empire. He was succeeded by some impressive rulers, including Akbar (reigned 1556–1605), a great warrior who also improved administration and allowed Hindus to once again worship freely, and Shah Jahan (reigned 1628–1658), who was responsible for the building of the Taj Mahal in Agra and the Red Fort in Delhi. Guru Nanak founded the Sikh religion in the sixteenth century in opposition to certain aspects of Mughal rule, notably the caste system.

Mughal power effectively came to an end after a crushing defeat at the hands of the Persians under Nader Shah in 1739, and the last Mughal emperor, Bahadur Shah II, died in exile in 1862, having been ousted by the British for his part in the Indian Rebellion of 1857.

Colonialism (sixteenth to eighteenth century)

Driven by the need for new trade routes beyond Europe that did not involve crossing the lands of the Ottoman empire to the east, Portugal led the way at the start of the sixteenth century by finding sea routes to the East Indies and Americas, and by establishing trading stations in Goa, Mozambique and Macao. Spain was next up, with her conquests in the West Indies and Central and South America bringing her untold riches.

By the seventeenth century, the Dutch, the French and the English decided they wanted a piece of the action. The Dutch set up the very profitable Dutch

East India Company, establishing trading posts in South Africa, South Asia and the Far East, and the equally lucrative Dutch West India Company, with trading posts in the West Indies and South America. The French grabbed huge amounts of land in North America (including Canada), the Caribbean and India, while the English set themselves up in India, the West Indies and North America, including the founding of the lucrative Hudson's Bay Company in Canada.

All of this greed for wealth and power led to one conflict after another around the world, not just between rival colonisers, but also between the colonisers and those who wanted to break free from the shackles they imposed. The most notable of those conflicts was the American Revolutionary War (1775–1783), also known as the American War of Independence, which did, of course, result in the independence that thirteen British colonies had long since declared for themselves on 4 July 1776.

The French Revolution (1789–1799)

In spite of demands for reform in the wake of Louis XIV's costly wars and lavish spending on the Palace of Versailles throughout his long reign (1643–1715), Louis XV and XVI succeeded him in similar vein, waging costly wars of their own and paying no taxes while the poor starved.

Years of suffering came to a head on 14 July 1789 when a mob stormed the Bastille in Paris, leading to a series of peasant revolts throughout the land. By 1792 the monarchy had been abolished and in 1793 Louis XVI and his wife Marie Antoinette were put to the guillotine. Things would probably have picked up a bit then, if only an extreme faction of the new government, the Jacobins under the control of Maximilien Robespierre, hadn't unleashed a 'Reign of Terror' of their own, executing around 40,000 peasants and workers over the course of the following year.

French Revolutionary Wars (1792–1802) and Napoleonic Wars (1803–1815)

The monarchies of Europe tried to teach Republican France a lesson by going to war with it in 1792 in the hope of restoring the French monarchy, but this only served to upset a young French general called Napoleon Bonaparte, who set about conquering the whole of Europe in order to teach it to mind its own business. He would probably have succeeded had it not been for a couple of severe naval defeats at the hands of Horatio Nelson in 1798 (Battle of the Nile) and 1805 (Battle of Trafalgar) and the fact that in 1812 he forgot just how cold the winter in Russia can get. He had one final go at fighting the whole of Europe in 1815, only to meet his Waterloo at the Battle of Waterloo.

The American Civil War (1861–1865)

When Abraham Lincoln was elected the sixteenth president of the United States in 1860, the southern states feared that he would abolish slavery and so they split from the Union to form a Confederacy. A brutal war ensued, in which 700,000 lives would be lost. In 1861, the Confederates gained the upper hand with a decisive victory at Manassas, Virginia under General 'Stonewall' Jackson and General Pierre Beauregard. In 1863, the

Union gained momentum after victory at the Battle of Gettysburg under Major General George Meade, and General William Sherman finished the Confederacy off with crushing victories at Atlanta and Savannah, Georgia in 1865, thereby compelling Confederate General Robert E. Lee to surrender to the Union's Commanding General Ulysses S. Grant.

The Scramble for Africa (1881–1914)

European exploration of the African interior in the nineteenth century provided knowledge about the rich, untapped resources that lay within, and we all know what that means, don't we? The scramble for Africa was on, and invasive colonisation was the name of the game across the African continent for the next thirty years or so. By the time the dust settled in 1914 and the Europeans had to get home to fight the First World War, only two African countries remained independent states: Abyssinia (present-day Ethiopia), which managed to see off the Italians; and Liberia, which was off limits because it had earlier been established as a free state for liberated (hence 'Liberia') Black American slaves.

The First World War (1914–1918)

In the early twentieth century there were so many treaties and pacts between the different nations of the world that it only needed a single event to create the domino effect that would give rise to global conflict. That single event was the assassination of Archduke Franz Ferdinand of Austria by Yugoslav nationalist Gavrilo Princep in Sarajevo on 28 June 1914. The domino effect resulted in the mobilisation of around 70 million military personnel, the horrors of trench warfare and around 16–18 million deaths. The victorious Allies consisted of the British Empire, the Russian Empire, France, Italy, Japan, the USA and several other smaller countries. The defeated Central Powers consisted of Germany, Austria-Hungary, Bulgaria and the Ottoman Empire.

When it was over, it was declared to be the war to end all wars and the League of Nations was formed to prevent such a catastrophic event ever happening again. It failed to meet its objective.

The Second World War (1939–1945)

Just 21 years after the war to end all wars, even more of the world's nations mobilised even more military personnel (around 100 million) in order to conduct the deadliest conflict in history. Estimates of the total number of deaths range from 50 to 85 million, and man's inhumanity to man reached new heights with the Holocaust and the bombing of whole cities, including the atomic bombings of Hiroshima and Nagasaki in Japan, which finally brought the war to an end.

The main theatres of war were Europe (notably the Battle of Britain aerial conflict, the Blitz bombing campaign and the D-Day landings of the Allies in northern France), North and East Africa, the Soviet Union, the Balkan countries, South East Asia, the Far East and the Atlantic and Pacific Oceans.

The victorious Allies consisted of 25 nations worldwide, the most significant protagonists being the United Kingdom, the USA, the Soviet Union, China and the ANZAC forces of Australia and New Zealand. The defeated Axis powers consisted only of Germany, Japan and Italy, although they did subjugate a further 23 countries worldwide to support their war effort.

Following the surrender of Germany (8 May 1945) and Japan (15 August 1945) at the end of the war, the League of Nations was replaced by the United Nations, which has been doing its level best ever since to prevent the many conflicts that continue to rage around the world from escalating into a third World War.

The Cold War (1947–1991)

Once the euphoria of victory in the Second World War had died down, the dictatorship of the Soviet Union and the democratic republic of the USA found themselves in bed together as 'world policemen'. It wasn't long before they realised what strange bedfellows they were and political and military tensions soon escalated as they flexed their muscles as the world's new superpowers. English writer George Orwell had foreseen this state of tension in October 1945 when he referred to the coming 'cold war' in a newspaper article.

In the decades that followed, a nuclear arms race promised mutually assured destruction and it was even thought that global domination awaited the eventual winner of the space race which ran in parallel. A number of proxy wars were fought in Greece, China, Korea, Egypt, Vietnam and Afghanistan. Psychological warfare, widespread espionage and the tense stand-offs of the Suez Crisis in 1956 and the Cuban Missile Crisis in 1962 kept the tension at boiling point.

Tensions eased with the Strategic Arms Limitation Talks (SALT) in the 1970s, and Soviet leader Mikhail Gorbachev went the extra mile in the 1980s when he introduced the liberal reforms of *glasnost* (openness) and *perestroika* (reorganisation) and ended Soviet involvement in Afghanistan. A wave of (mostly) peaceful revolutions followed in Eastern Europe, leading to the collapse of the Berlin Wall in 1989 and the dissolution of the Soviet Union in 1991.

British modern history

All the while this stuff was going on around the world over the last 500 years or so, Britain was cracking on with its royal dynasties, so let's get back to them. To begin with, the Tudor dynasty settled in under Henry VII, who spent his 24-year reign (1485–1509) returning the country to prosperity and order following the unsettling period of the Wars of the Roses. He was so successful as a ruler that he was able to leave a fortune and a relatively sound system of government to his son, King Henry VIII. What could possibly go wrong?

House of Tudor (1485–1603):

Henry VII (1485–1509)
Henry VIII (1509–1547)

Edward VI (1547–1553)
Lady Jane Grey (1553)
Mary I (1553–1558)
Elizabeth I (1558–1603)

Eventful stuff of the Tudor era

Henry VIII worked his way through six wives and dissolved the monasteries after the Pope refused to recognise the annulment of his marriage to Catherine of Aragon.

The sickly Edward VI became king at the age of nine and died at the ripe old age of 15. His advisors had tried to get him married to the teenage Mary, Queen of Scots, but her advisors had preferred to align with France.

Bloody Mary (Mary I) had a teenage rival for the throne (Lady Jane Grey) executed, had Protestants persecuted and burned on a fearsome scale and just stopped short of having her half-sister Elizabeth executed. She did make a nice cocktail, though.

Elizabeth I reinstated Protestantism, encouraged exploration of the New World by the likes of Francis Drake and Walter Raleigh, allowed the arts to flourish (Shakespeare was a particular favourite and the Globe Theatre was opened during her reign) and drank two pints of beer for breakfast.

Mary, Queen of Scots got her head chopped off in 1587 for being too Catholic, too French (she had in fact been Queen of France for a while and French was her first language) and too conspiratorial (she longed for the hat trick of being Queen of Scotland, France and England).

In 1588 the Spanish Armada was defeated by a combination of English ships and English weather.

The six wives of Henry VIII

Here are the results of Henry VIII's six marriages:

Catherine of Aragon	Divorced	Produced the future Mary I, but had to go after failing to produce a son and heir.
Anne Boleyn	Beheaded	Produced the future Elizabeth I, but also failed to bear a son and was allegedly a bit too popular with the boys around court in any event.
Jane Seymour	Died	Lost her life giving birth to the future Edward VI, and would otherwise probably have lived happily ever after with Henry after giving him the male heir he always wanted.
Anne of Cleves	Divorced	Described by Henry as the 'mare of Flanders', she was removed for being insufficiently pleasing to the eye.

| Catherine Howard | Beheaded | Another one who allegedly put it about too much at court, which was so embarrassing it earned her a beheading. |
| Catherine Parr | Survived | After three other marriages of her own, she managed Henry and looked after his children so well that she survived long enough to outlive him. |

House of Stuart (1603–1714)

James I (1603–1625)
Charles I (1625–1649)
Charles II (1660–1685)
James II (1685–1688)
William III and Mary II (1689–1702)
Anne (1702–1714)

Eventful stuff of the Stuart era

The court turned all Scottish in 1603 when James VI of Scotland (the son of Mary, Queen of Scots) also became James I of England. James and his courtiers brought their golf clubs down to London with them (the game had already been played in Scotland for around 150 years) and in no time the game became just as popular down south.

On 5 November 1605, Catholic dissidents, including Guy Fawkes, tried to blow up the House of Lords during the State Opening of Parliament by King James.

Charles I had his head removed in 1649 after being scornful and dismissive of Parliament once too often.

After the Parliamentarian Roundheads defeated the Royalist Cavaliers in the English Civil War (1642–1651), the miserable Oliver Cromwell ruled as Lord Protector of the Commonwealth for the next decade or so. Even Christmas was banned under his fun-hating regime.

In 1660 the monarchy was restored when the Merry Monarch (Charles II) returned from exile in France. Christmas was immediately reinstated, along with general merriment and debauchery at court.

The Great Plague of 1665 and the Great Fire of London in 1666 spoiled the ongoing party a bit. The Great Plague took out around 100,000 people, about a quarter of the population of London at the time. The Great Fire killed only a handful of people, but destroyed 87 parish churches, St Paul's Cathedral and over 13,000 homes, leaving most of the inner-city population homeless. On the plus side, the Great Fire put paid to any chance of the Great Plague flaring up again.

William III of Orange and his wife (and cousin) Queen Mary restored some sobriety to the court in 1689. That same year, the Bill of Rights was passed to limit the powers of the crown, allow parliament to hold regular elections and practise free speech, allow Protestants to bear arms to defend themselves, and stipulate that no Catholic could accede to the throne.

The 1707 Acts of Union brought Scotland and England together under the single monarchy of Queen Anne to form the Kingdom of Great Britain.

When Queen Anne died in 1714 her body was so swollen with gout that she had to be buried in an almost square coffin.

House of Hanover (1714–1901)

George I (1714–1727)
George II (1727–1760)
George III (1760–1820)
George IV (1820–1830)
William IV (1830–1837)
Victoria (1837–1901)

Eventful stuff of the Hanoverian era

George I turned up to rule Britain speaking only German and soon became the subject of ridicule. His two mistresses were dubbed 'Maypole' and 'Elephant and Castle' by the satirists of the day (one was said to resemble a stick insect, while the other was apparently obese).

The Seven Years' War (1754–1763) was in fact the main phase of a nine years' war that resulted in Britain taking control of French Canada (after General James Wolfe took Quebec), Spanish Florida and Bengal in East India (mainly thanks to the efforts of the British commander Robert Clive).

During the reign of George III, Britain lost the American Wars of Independence (1775–1783) but recovered to win the Napoleonic Wars (1803–1815). George took the American defeat very badly, even considering abdication, and later went quite mad before he could enjoy the subsequent victories against Napoleon.

George IV is mostly remembered for championing the Regency style of architecture, locking his wife Charlotte out of his coronation and getting fat. It is thought that he may well have inspired the nursery rhyme: 'Georgie Porgie, pudding and pie, kissed the girls and made them cry.'

The Abolition of Slavery Act was passed in 1833 thanks to Member of Parliament William Wilberforce and in spite of opposition from William IV.

STUFF AND NONSENSE

Serves them right

In eighteenth- and nineteenth-century Britain crimes that were actually punished by transportation to Australia included setting a haystack on fire, stealing gingham in Halifax (never a good idea), being an Irish rebel, stealing a hairbrush and escaping from transportation (which seems fair enough really).

Crimes punishable by death at the time, considered by many a lesser sentence than transportation to Australia, included impersonating a Chelsea pensioner, living with gypsies for a month and 'strong evidence of malice' in children aged 7–14.

During the Victorian age Britain became the industrial powerhouse of the world, producing vast quantities of steel, coal, iron and textiles. It was the age of the train and of the growth of cities.

Although America had been lost, Britain still had Canada, Australia, New Zealand, India, many parts of Africa and the Caribbean and much more besides. Victoria was said to reign over an empire on which the sun never set, ruling over a quarter of the world's population and landmass (but she remained against women's rights, presumably because she already had all the rights she needed).

Victorian firsts included the postage stamp, telegraph, telephone, free schooling, trade unions and Greenwich Mean Time (GMT).

House of Saxe-Coburg and Gotha (1901–1910)

Edward VII (1901–1910)

Eventful stuff of the Saxe-Coburg and Gotha era

Edward VII had enjoyed a playboy lifestyle as Prince of Wales while waiting for his mother's reign to finally end. He particularly enjoyed horse racing, shooting, fine wines, actresses (especially Lillie Langtry) and other men's wives.

As monarch, Edward VII modernised the armed forces and personally promoted the Entente Cordiale signed with France in 1904 to rule out future wars between England and France.

Strictly speaking, George V was a monarch of the House of Saxe-Coburg and Gotha for the first seven years of his reign, until he changed the family name to Windsor (see below).

House of Windsor (1910–present)

George V (1910–1936)
Edward VIII (1936)
George VI (1936–1952)
Elizabeth II (1952–)

Eventful stuff of the Windsor era

George V had the horrific burden of the First World War to contend with and made several visits to the front line. In 1917 he wisely changed the family name from Saxe-Coburg and Gotha to Windsor and relinquished all German ties.

In 1913 the Suffragette movement gained ground after Emily Davison threw herself under King George V's horse at the Epsom Derby. In 1919 Lady Astor became the first female MP and by 1928 all women over 21 had the vote.

The Spanish Flu epidemic of 1918 killed around 50 million people worldwide, 4 per cent of the world's population and around three times the number killed in the First World War.

In 1922 George V sent a ship to rescue the Greek royal family from revolutionaries. On board was the one-year-old Prince Philip, who would go on to become the Duke of Edinburgh.

On 10 December 1936, Edward VIII abdicated the throne in favour of marrying Wallis Simpson, a twice-married American woman and therefore of the wrong stock for royalty entirely.

Known as Albert until his accession in 1936, George VI overcame a speech impediment to reign in the place of his abdicated brother. He witnessed the horrors of the Second World War, but he and his wife Queen Elizabeth refused to leave London during the Blitz.

In addition to defeating Adolf Hitler's Nazi Germany in the Second World War, Winston Churchill won the Nobel Prize for Literature in 1953 and entered the music charts with a collection of his greatest speeches just after his death in 1965, and again in 2010 when his speeches were set to music to commemorate the seventieth anniversary of the Battle of Britain (both records are still available on iTunes).

The British Empire gave way to the Commonwealth of Nations in 1949 as country after country gained independence. Today the Commonwealth has 53 member nations, with Queen Elizabeth II at its head in addition to remaining the head of state of 16 of the nations. Five member nations have their own monarch (Brunei, Lesotho, Malaysia, Swaziland and Tonga) and the rest are republics. Mozambique and Rwanda have been admitted as members in spite of not ever having had any colonial or constitutional ties with the UK.

The Troubles in Northern Ireland ran for 30 years (1968–1998), the main issue being whether the country should remain part of the UK or join the Irish Republic. It ultimately resulted in a power-sharing self-government within the Northern Ireland Assembly.

Under the leadership of its first female prime minister, Margaret Thatcher, Britain retook the Falkland Islands after an Argentinian invasion in 1982.

Scotland and Wales voted in favour of having their own parliaments in 1997.

Elizabeth II became the longest-ever reigning British monarch on 9 September 2015, finally overtaking her great great-grandmother Queen Victoria after 63 years, 7 months and 3 days on the throne.

POSITIVE HISTORY

History is full of war, plague and human rights abuses of one kind or another, so it's important to remind ourselves about some of its more positive events so that we don't lose faith in the human race entirely. Here are some such events to lift our spirits:

In the face of oppression and brutality on the part of the British Raj, Mahatma Gandhi secured independence for India in 1947 after years of peaceful protest, non-cooperation and self-deprivation.

American civil rights leader Martin Luther King Jr paved the way to racial equality in the USA with his non-violent opposition to segregation and his famous 'I have a dream' speech on 28 August 1963. Delivered to a mass crowd of 250,000 protestors at the Lincoln Memorial in Washington, D.C., his words soon reverberated around the world. He was assassinated in 1968, after which a long campaign began to have a federal holiday named after him. The campaign proved successful in 1986, since which time the date of his birthday, 15 January, has been celebrated nationally as Martin Luther King Jr Day.

The people of Estonia, Latvia and Lithuania demonstrated their solidarity in the desire for independence from Soviet Russia when two million of them held hands on 23 August 1989 in order to form a human chain across all three countries. The so-called Baltic Chain stretched for over 650 km (about 400 miles).

After 27 years in prison (on Robben Island for 18 years, Pollsmoor Prison for 6 years and Victor Verster Prison for 2 years) for protesting against South African apartheid, Nelson Mandela showed an extraordinary amount of forgiveness when he emerged in 1990 to work for a better future for blacks and whites alike. He spent five years as the country's first black president, forming a multi-ethnic government to ensure a peaceful transition.

In 1984 musicians Bob Geldof and Midge Ure pressganged the good and the great of the music industry into recording the charity single 'Do They Know It's Christmas?' in order to raise funds for an ongoing famine in Ethiopia. It shot to number one and quickly raised £8 million. Spurred on by this success, they organised the 1985 Live Aid concert simultaneously at Wembley Stadium in London and John F. Kennedy Stadium in Philadelphia. The concert ultimately raised £150 million and was watched by nearly two billion people across 150 countries.

Other hugely successful fundraising events in recent times include three 'telethons': Red Nose Day and Sport Relief in support of the Comic Relief charity and the BBC's Children in Need. Comic Relief has raised over £1 billion in 30 years and Children in Need has raised over £600 million.

Aung San Suu Kyi spent 15 years over a 21-year period under house arrest for speaking out against the iron-fisted rule of Myanmar's military dictatorship. She was allowed to leave the country at any time to rejoin her English husband and children, but she refused, determined instead to make a stand for democracy and human rights. In 2010 she was finally released and her democratic party has since been swept to power.

STUFF AND NONSENSE

'Dear Manuel, sorry to hear you got deposed.'

A ten-year-old American girl called Sarah York started writing to the Panamanian dictator Manuel Noriega after her father encouraged her to do so because she liked the dictator's hat. She and Noriega became pen pals, which resulted in her and her family going for a holiday in Panama, where they were given a guided tour under military escort. A year later, in 1989, the USA invaded Panama and deposed Noriega.

A BIT OF CULTURE

INTRODUCTION

A little bit of culture does us good. It broadens the mind and allows us to escape from whatever we need to escape from. The many types of culture to choose from range from classic literature and the paintings of the old masters to modern-day soap operas and reality television.

The social scene is also more wide-ranging than ever, with cafe society sitting alongside fast-food chains and ultra-trendy restaurants with prices to match. You can even stay in tune with the entire world without getting off your backside these days, thanks to the ubiquitous availability of social media, online shopping and celebrity-stalking opportunities. But you still can't beat a good book, so let's start there.

LITERATURE

Ever since the first printing press of Johannes Gutenberg was introduced in Germany in 1440, literature has been enlightening and entertaining greater numbers of people than the ancient storytellers or parchment writers could possibly have imagined. It has become increasingly available to the masses, to the extent that we can now download whole books to an electronic reader within seconds.

Leaving aside the Koran, the Bible and Chairman Mao's *Little Red Book*, which probably all sold in their billions before records began to be kept, the ten top-selling books of all time are as follows:

The Lord of the Rings (1955)	J. R. R. Tolkien	150 m
The Hobbit (1937)	J. R. R. Tolkien	142 m
Le Petit Prince (1943)	Antoine de Saint-Exupéry	140 m
Harry Potter and the Philosopher's Stone (1997)	J. K. Rowling	107 m
And Then There Were None (1939)	Agatha Christie	100 m
Dream of the Red Chamber (1791)	Cao Xueqin	100 m
She: A History of Adventure (1887)	H. Rider Haggard	100 m
The Lion, the Witch and the Wardrobe (1950)	C. S. Lewis	85 m
The Da Vinci Code (2003)	Dan Brown	80 m
Think and Grow Rich (1937)	Napoleon Hill	70 m

Loitering just outside the top ten are J. K. Rowling's *Harry Potter and the Half-blood Prince*, J. D. Salinger's *The Catcher in the Rye* and Paulo Coelho's *The Alchemist*.

In addition to the Koran, the Bible and the jottings of Chairman Mao, there are a number of other older books that would probably be candidates for the top ten if only they had reliable sales figures. These include:

Iliad and *Odyssey* (8th century BCE)	Homer
Don Quixote (1615)	Miguel de Cervantes
Pride and Prejudice (1813)	Jane Austen
The Three Musketeers (1844)	Alexandre Dumas
A Tale of Two Cities (1859)	Charles Dickens
Les Misérables (1862)	Victor Hugo
Alice's Adventures in Wonderland (1865)	Lewis Carroll
The Adventures of Pinocchio (1883)	Carlo Collodi

The best-selling book *series* of all time is, unsurprisingly, J. K. Rowling's *Harry Potter*, followed by R. L. Stine's *Goosebumps*, Erle Stanley Gardner's *Perry Mason*, and Stan and Jan Berenstain's *Berenstain Bears*.

The best-selling authors of all time are William Shakespeare and Agatha Christie, both estimated to have sales of around four billion, which is three billion more than third-placed Barbara Cartland (who dictated all of her novels to a secretary while reclined on a sofa with a white fur rug and a hot-water bottle).

Phrases originally coined by Shakespeare

Here are but a few of the hundreds of phrases that would not be in common use today if William Shakespeare had not thought them up during the course of his writing:

The world's my oyster	*The Merry Wives of Windsor*
Refuse to budge an inch	*The Taming of the Shrew*
The milk of human kindness	*Macbeth*
Dead as a doornail	*Henry VI Part 2*
Elbow room	*King John*
For goodness' sake	*Henry VIII*
It was all Greek to me	*Julius Caesar*
Foregone conclusion	*Othello*
Good riddance	*Troilus and Cressida*
Wild goose chase	*Romeo and Juliet*
Too much of a good thing	*As You Like It*
Salad days	*Antony and Cleopatra*
One fell swoop	*Macbeth*
Not slept a wink	*Cymbeline*
Jealousy is the green-eyed monster	*Othello*
Love is blind	*The Merchant of Venice*
In a pickle	*The Tempest*
Heart of gold	*Henry V*
Wear your heart on your sleeve	*Othello*
The be-all and end-all	*Macbeth*

It is also estimated that Shakespeare created around 1,700 new words that are still in common use today. If, for example, you say that 'the art of barefaced hobnobbing is obscene enough to make you puke', you pretty much owe the whole sentence to the Bard.

STUFF AND NONSENSE

Uneasy lies the body without a head

An archaeological scan of William Shakespeare's grave in Stratford-upon-Avon has revealed that his skull is missing, lending credence to the long-held theory that trophy hunters removed it in 1794. It may be much ado about nothing, but I like to think it's still starring somewhere as Yorick in stage productions of *Hamlet*.

A few surprising literary facts

In response to a bet in 1960 that he couldn't write a book using no more than 50 different words, the American writer and illustrator Dr Seuss (pronounced Zoice) did just that. *Green Eggs and Ham* went on to become one of the top selling children's books of all time.

The best-selling novel ever in France was not written by Victor Hugo, Guy de Maupassant, Georges Simenon or any of its other home-grown literary greats. It is in fact *The Da Vinci Code*, written by American author Dan Brown, and it has been read by over a quarter of the country's population.

English writer Ian Fleming is best known for his James Bond spy novels, but he also wrote the best-selling children's book *Chitty-Chitty-Bang-Bang*, since adapted for film, theatre and radio.

Leo Tolstoy's wife Sophia wrote out seven drafts of *War and Peace* for him, in longhand.

The Brontë sisters originally wrote under pseudonyms due to a prejudice against female writers in nineteenth-century Britain. They did at least manage to maintain their own initials, though.

Author	Pseudonym	Most famous novel
Charlotte Brontë	Currer Bell	*Jane Eyre*
Emily Brontë	Ellis Bell	*Wuthering Heights*
Anne Brontë	Acton Bell	*The Tenant of Wildfell Hall*

The best-selling Finnish magazine in Finland is the weekly comic *Aku Ankka*, aka Walt Disney's Donald Duck, which is now more popular in Finland than in the USA, its country of origin.

A mobile library uses camels to deliver books (400 per camel) to schools and nomadic tribes in the remotest regions of Kenya.

In 1956 American author Harper Lee was given a year's wages by her friends as a Christmas present. She spent the year writing *To Kill a Mockingbird*.

Ernest Hemingway's dreadful mother (she sometimes dressed him as a girl alongside his sister when he was growing up) was so ashamed of his novel *The Sun Also Rises* that she refused to go to her book club when it was being discussed.

Guinness World Records holds the world record for being the book most often stolen from public libraries.

In the Carlo Collodi novel that the much milder film *Pinocchio* was based on, Pinocchio had his feet burned off and was hanged. Served him right for telling lies.

MUSIC

Music has always played an important part in human life and today we are privileged to enjoy an immense back catalogue stretching back hundreds of years.

Classical music

Music as we know it today really took off in the seventeenth and eighteenth centuries, during the Baroque period of great composers like Vivaldi, Bach, Handel and Pachelbel. The Classical period of the eighteenth century brought us the likes of Haydn, Mozart, Beethoven and Schubert, and the Romantic music of the nineteenth century delivered Chopin, Strauss (father and son), Tchaikovsky, Brahms, Liszt and many more besides.

The brilliance and diversity of Mozart popularised opera in Germany and beyond, and great Italian composers like Verdi, Puccini and Rossini brought it to the masses in such a powerful way that opera remains an intrinsic part of life in Italy to this day and continues to be popular around the world.

Modern music

The twentieth century saw a total revolution as radio brought music to the masses and new media were developed to capture, record and distribute existing and new genres. The choice became quite staggering, from classical and opera to folk, pop and rock, from electronic, disco and hip hop to blues, country and jazz. Each new generation wanted its own musical identity and transient styles like punk, rave, house and garage came and went.

The available media progressed through gramophone, vinyl, tape, compact disc and MP3 to arrive at the present age of downloads and streaming services like Spotify, Apple Music, Deezer, Amazon Prime Music, Tidal and Pandora, while live music reached the dizzy heights of superstar DJs, arena tours and festival weekends. In a multibillion-pound industry, you have to shift a few copies to reach the top of the musical tree these days. In terms of total sales, there is no prize for guessing that the Beatles remain number one, with 270 million sales and still growing. According to certified sales figures regularly supplied by the music industry (as opposed to claimed sales by artists), here are the top 25 best sellers of all time:

Performer(s)	Nationality	Sales (approx.)
The Beatles	British	270 million
Elvis Presley	American	211 million
Rihanna	Barbadian	197 million
Michael Jackson	American	180 million
Madonna	American	170 million
Elton John	British	167 million
Taylor Swift	American	147 million
Garth Brooks	American	144 million
Led Zeppelin	British	139 million
Mariah Carey	American	132 million
Eagles	American	129 million
Céline Dion	Canadian	124 million
Eminem	American	123 million

Performer(s)	Nationality	Sales (approx.)
Pink Floyd	British	118 million
Katy Perry	American	117 million
AC/DC	Australian	112 million
Whitney Houston	American	112 million
Queen	British	109 million
U2	Irish	106 million
Billy Joel	American	102 million
Bruce Springsteen	American	100 million
Kanye West	American	100 million
Barbra Streisand	American	97 million
The Rolling Stones	British	95 million
Lady Gaga	American	95 million

The best-selling album of all time is *Thriller* (Michael Jackson, 1982) and the best-selling single of all time is *White Christmas* (Bing Crosby, 1942).

A few surprising music facts

Lisztomania broke out in Berlin in 1841, preceding Beatlemania by 120 years. The object of the frenzy was Hungarian composer Franz Liszt, who was supposedly the first musician to have women's underwear thrown at him while performing on stage.

Mozart's big sister Marianne was also a musician and usually took top billing when they toured Europe together as child prodigies.

None of the Beatles could read or write music. When Paul McCartney wrote his symphony *Standing Stone*, he did it on a computer rigged to transcribe the music he played into sheet music.

When Don McLean wrote and sang about 'the day the music died' in his 1972 hit single 'American Pie', he was referring to the day that Buddy Holly died in a plane crash in 1959, along with Ritchie Valens and J. P. Richardson Jr, aka The Big Bopper. Other famous musicians to die in plane crashes include bandleader Glenn Miller (1944, when his plane disappeared over the English Channel), country singer Jim Reeves (1964), soul singer Otis Redding (1967), folk singer John Denver (1997) and R & B singer Aaliyah (2001).

Barry Manilow's number one hit 'I Write the Songs' wasn't written by Barry Manilow.

The Gallagher brothers named the band Oasis after spotting the name of a tour venue on an Inspiral Carpets poster in their bedroom: the Oasis Leisure Centre in Swindon.

The Eurovision Song Contest has been going strong for over 60 years and it remains Europe's most popular TV show year after year. Here is some stuff you may or may not know about it:

- Swedish supergroup Abba shot to fame after winning the 1974 contest in Brighton.
- When Israel won in 1978, Jordanian television showed a bunch of flowers during their performance and later pretended that Belgium (who had come second) had won.
- Canadian singing superstar Céline Dion won the competition in 1988, singing in French and representing Switzerland.
- Equally successful as a social activist and a singer/musician, Ruslana won the 2004 contest with a song devoted to the Orange Revolution taking place within Ukraine at the time. She went on to become a member of the Ukrainian parliament, a UNICEF Goodwill Ambassador and an International Woman of Courage (conferred annually by the USA to honour women who have made a difference by promoting human rights).
- When Engelbert Humperdinck represented Britain at the 2012 Eurovision Song Contest, he wasn't just the oldest contestant at the age of 76, he was older than many of the countries taking part.

- The contest has such a massive fan base Down Under that Australia was invited to join in 2015, coming a respectable fifth on their first appearance.
- The host country is traditionally the country that won the previous year, but on four occasions the UK has hosted the event because the previous year's winner couldn't afford to do so.
- Before the UK's long run of poor results since 1999, it was hugely successful, winning on five occasions and finishing runner-up 15 times. The five winning entries were as follows:

  - 'Puppet on a String': Sandie Shaw (1967)
  - 'Boom Bang-a-Bang': Lulu (1969)
  - 'Save Your Kisses for Me': Brotherhood of Man (1976)
  - 'Making Your Mind Up': Bucks Fizz (1981)
  - 'Love Shine a Light': Katrina and the Waves (1997)

STUFF AND NONSENSE

Karaoke

Karaoke is Japanese for 'empty orchestra' and there are over 100,000 karaoke bars in China. Karaoke world championships have been held since 2003 at venues as diverse as Killarney in Ireland and on board the MS *Galaxy* ferry as it sailed back and forth between Helsinki in Finland and Tallinn in Estonia. As a form of entertainment, karaoke is today a billion-dollar industry, but it's not popular with everyone. It has been the cause of a number of deaths in the Philippines known as the 'My Way' killings, all perpetrated by customers who just couldn't take one more rendition of the song popularised by Frank Sinatra.

ART

Whether your thing is the art of the old Dutch masters or the French Impressionists or Tracey Emin's unmade bed, here are a few arty facts that might have you popping off to the gallery or reaching for your easel:

In 1508, Michelangelo accepted the commission to paint the ceiling of the Sistine Chapel with great reluctance as he considered himself a sculptor by trade and had never painted a fresco before. He endured four years of physical torture and a paint-splattered face before emerging victorious in 1512.

Leonardo da Vinci worked on the *Mona Lisa* for 15 years and didn't consider it finished when he died in 1519. That might explain the absence of eyebrows on her face.

When the *Mona Lisa* was stolen from the Louvre museum in Paris in 1911, one of the suspects was Pablo Picasso.

In 1539, Henry VIII agreed to marry Anne of Cleves based on a portrait provided by his court painter Hans Holbein the Younger. Holbein was lucky to keep his head on his shoulders after Henry declared the real Anne to be rather less attractive than the portrait had suggested.

The seventeenth-century Flemish painter Peter Paul Rubens became famous for his paintings of full-bodied women, hence the enduring term Rubenesque to describe an aptly endowed figure.

Dutch painter Johannes Vermeer struggled to make ends meet during his lifetime in seventeenth-century Delft and could have done with Hollywood knocking on the door a bit sooner to encapsulate his life in *Girl with a Pearl Earring*, the 2003 film starring Colin Firth and Scarlett Johansson. As it was, the now priceless painting was sold at auction in 1881 for two guilders and 30 cents – about £20 in today's money.

English painter J. M. W. Turner was a master of colour and light, which he used to great effect in portraying landscapes, maritime scenes and weather. One of his most famous paintings, *The Fighting Temeraire*, will be appearing behind him on the reverse of the Bank of England's new £20 note, due to be in circulation, rather appropriately, by 2020.

In 1891 Claude Monet won 100,000 francs (about the equivalent of £8,000 today) in the French lottery, allowing him to quit his job and concentrate on perfecting his Impressionist style.

Encouraged by his parents, the Spanish surrealist painter and egomaniac Salvador Dalí believed he was the reincarnation of his older brother, who was also called Salvador and had died nine months before the new Salvador was unveiled to the world in 1904.

The American abstract expressionist painter Jackson Pollock used a technique called 'drip painting' to create his chaotically colourful canvasses.

Norwegian artist Edvard Munch created five versions of *The Scream*, four different painted or pastel versions plus a stone lithograph. One of the four painted versions fetched just under $120 million at auction in 2012.

Le Bateau, a paper-cut created by French artist Henri Matisse, hung upside down in the Museum of Modern Art in New York for 47 days in 1961 until a visitor noticed the mistake.

The Starry Night was painted by Vincent Van Gogh from a window of the asylum he admitted himself to in Saint-Rémy-de-Provence in 1889, not long after he had cut off part of his left ear. He painted one 'star' much brighter than the rest and research has since confirmed that the planet Venus was particularly visible and bright in southern Provence at the time.

If you want to sound really clever on your next trip to a museum or art gallery, or perhaps just trick your parents into thinking that your education wasn't a complete waste of time and money, here is some great jargon on a few of the many art movements that have sprung up over the centuries:

Art movement (dates are approximate)	Jargon to make you sound clever
Stone Age (30000–2500 BCE)	'I love what they've done with their cave.'
Classical (fifth to fourth century BCE)	'What perfectly proportioned columns! I'm pretty sure they're either Doric, Ionic or Corinthian.'
Byzantine and Islamic (476–1453 CE)	'Amazing mosaics. They remind me of the Alhambra palace in Granada.'
Medieval (500–1500)	'Do you prefer the French Gothic of Notre Dame or the Gothic Revival of the Tower of London?'
Renaissance (1400–1550)	Just recite the names of the four Teenage Mutant Ninja Turtles. Donatello, Michelangelo, Raphael and Leonardo (da Vinci), and throw in the phrase 'more realistic than ever before'.

Art movement (dates are approximate)	Jargon to make you sound clever
Mannerism (1527–1580)	'I love the way that Michelangelo threw away the rule book towards the end with his exaggerated figures on the ceiling of the Sistine Chapel, and don't even get me started on the proportions of his statue of David!'
Baroque (1600–1750)	'Does greater splendour exist outside the Palace of Versailles? I don't think so.'
Neoclassical (1760–1850)	'I recognise a return to the symmetry of the Ancient Greeks and Romans. No wonder the Grand Tour became so popular with the landed gentry.'
Romanticism (1780–1850)	'I love the emotion and individuality of this period. We really must visit the Turner Contemporary gallery in Margate.'
Pre-Raphaelite (1848–1860)	'A return to the morality of the Renaissance before that Raphael got a bit carried away.'
Realism (1848–1900)	'Seeing the peasants and working classes going about their everyday lives makes me feel quite humble.'

Art movement (dates are approximate)	Jargon to make you sound clever
Impressionism (1865–1885)	'Monet kick-started this movement with his portrayal of the effect of light on the French landscape.'
Post-Impressionism (1885–1905)	'The use of strong form and colour was positively industrial compared to the softness of the Impressionists.'
Art Nouveau (1890–1910)	'I think Charles Rennie Mackintosh took the Arts and Crafts of William Morris to a new level.'
Expressionism (1900–1935)	'It's just so subjective. We each have to find our own levels of angst when we look at Munch's *The Scream*.'
Cubism (1905–1920)	'I think this is when Picasso abandoned realism to concentrate on the solidity of volume.'
Surrealism (1917–1950)	'I think Salvador Dalí was just ridiculous, but in a good way.'
Abstract Expressionism (1943–1965)	'Once you've figured out which way up a Rothko or Pollock is meant to be looked at, they really draw you in.'

Art movement (dates are approximate)	Jargon to make you sound clever
Pop Art (1955–1970)	'I love the comic-book appeal of Warhol's portrayal of celebrity culture and mass advertising.'
Postmodernism (1970s–)	'So experimental and innovative. Anything goes, really.'

FILM AND THEATRE

Film is a relative newcomer when you consider that theatre has been on the go since ancient times. In spite of the fact that film has blossomed from the humble beginnings of its silent-movie era at the turn of the twentieth century into the multibillion-dollar industry that it is today, though, theatre remains surprisingly alive and well alongside it. Let's have a look at the highest-grossing films of all time and the longest-running plays ever in London's West End before we enjoy some entertaining entertainment trivia.

Highest-grossing films of all time (adjusted for inflation)

Film	Director	Stars	Adjusted takings (US$)
Gone with the Wind (1939)	Victor Fleming	Clark Gable, Vivien Leigh, Leslie Howard, Olivia de Havilland	3.4 billion
Avatar (2009)	James Cameron	Sam Worthington, Zoe Saldana, Stephen Lang, Michelle Rodriguez, Sigourney Weaver	3.0 billion
Star Wars: Episode IV – A New Hope (1977)	George Lucas	Mark Hamill, Harrison Ford, Carrie Fisher, Peter Cushing, Alec Guinness	2.8 billion
Titanic (1997)	James Cameron	Leonardo DiCaprio, Kate Winslet	2.5 billion

Film	Director	Stars	Adjusted takings (US$)
The Sound of Music (1965)	Robert Wise	Julie Andrews, Christopher Plummer	2.4 billion
E.T. the Extra-Terrestrial (1982)	Steven Spielberg	Henry Thomas, Drew Barrymore, Dee Wallace, Peter Coyote, Robert MacNaughton	2.3 billion
The Ten Commandments (1956)	Cecil B. DeMille	Charlton Heston, Yul Brynner, Anne Baxter, Edward G. Robinson, Yvonne de Carlo, Debra Paget, John Derek	2.2 billion
Doctor Zhivago (1965)	David Lean	Omar Sharif, Julie Christie, Tom Courtenay, Alec Guinness, Geraldine Chaplin, Rod Steiger	2.1 billion

Film	Director	Stars	Adjusted takings (US$)
Jaws (1975)	Steven Spielberg	Roy Scheider, Robert Shaw, Richard Dreyfuss, Lorraine Gary, Murray Hamilton	2.0 billion
Snow White and the Seven Dwarfs (1937)	William Cottrell, David Hand	Adriana Caselotti, Harry Stockwell (voices only, as this was an animated film)	1.8 billion

Longest-running plays in London's West End

London West End production	Script, music and/or lyrics	Length of run (as of 2016)
The Mousetrap (1952)	Agatha Christie	64 years
Les Misérables (1985)	Claude-Michel Schönberg, Alain Boublil, Jean-Marc Natel	31 years
The Phantom of the Opera (1986)	Andrew Lloyd Webber, Charles Hart	30 years
The Woman in Black (1989)	Susan Hill, Stephen Mallatratt	27 years

Blood Brothers (1998–2012)	Willy Russell	24 years
Cats (1981–2002)	Andrew Lloyd Webber (based on T. S. Eliot's *Old Possum's Book of Practical Cats*)	21 years
Starlight Express (1984–2002)	Andrew Lloyd Webber, Richard Stilgoe	18 years
Mamma Mia! (1999)	Catherine Johnson, Benny Andersson, Björn Ulvaeus	17 years
The Lion King (1999)	Elton John, Tim Rice	17 years
No Sex Please, We're British (1971–1987)	Alistair Foot, Anthony Marriott	16 years

A few surprising film and theatre facts

The Mousetrap is the longest-running play in the world, with over 26,000 performances in London's West End and counting. It has been running continuously since 1952, when Richard Attenborough and his wife Sheila Sim were the stars of the show.

Most of the clocks in Quentin Tarantino's *Pulp Fiction* are stuck at 4:20.

The sound effects for the famous shower scene in Alfred Hitchcock's black-and-white 1960 film *Psycho* were created by the repeated stabbing of a melon, and chocolate syrup was used as blood.

The Hindi-language cinema industry known as Bollywood produces twice as many films as Hollywood and sells 3.5 billion tickets each year, about a billion more than Hollywood manages.

In Ancient Rome, if the script of a play required the death of an actor, a convicted murderer would be sent on in the place of the actor at the last minute. The live execution of the murderer gave the drama a degree of realism that is difficult to match these days.

In 1915 Charlie Chaplin entered a Charlie Chaplin lookalike competition and failed to make the final.

Richard Gere's middle name is Tiffany.

Brad Pitt injured his Achilles tendon while playing the part of Achilles in the film *Troy*, thereby delaying production for several weeks.

English actress Gemma Arterton was born with six fingers on each hand. Her extra fingers did fall off after the doctor who delivered her tied them off with sutures, but you can still see the scars if you look really closely and, let's be honest, there are worse things to look at really closely than Gemma Arterton.

Oscar Hammerstein II (of Rodgers and Hammerstein fame) is the only Oscar to ever win an Oscar (he won Best Original Song twice in the 1940s).

Most Academy Awards won

- Most awards won by a male: Walt Disney (22)
- Most awards won by a female: Edith Head (8) – all for costume design
- Most awards for directing: John Ford (4)
- Most awards for acting: Katherine Hepburn (4) – Meryl Streep, Jack Nicholson and Daniel Day-Lewis each need one more to draw level

Three films in history have picked up a staggering 11 Oscars:

- *Ben-Hur* (1959)
- *Titanic* (1997)
- *The Lord of the Rings: The Return of the King* (2003)

TELEVISION AND RADIO

In Britain, the most-watched TV programmes in history (excluding sporting events and news coverage) are as follows:

Programme	Viewers (approx.)	Date
EastEnders	30.2 million	25 December 1986
EastEnders	28.0 million	1 January 1986
Coronation Street	26.7 million	25 December 1987
Only Fools and Horses	24.4 million	29 December 1996
EastEnders	24.3 million	2 January 1992
Royal Variety Performance	24.2 million	14 November 1965
EastEnders	24.1 million	7 January 1988
To the Manor Born	24.0 million	11 November 1979
Miss World	23.8 million	19 November 1967
EastEnders	23.6 million	26 December 1985

The most-watched programme was the Christmas Day *EastEnders* episode where Dirty Den served divorce papers on his wife Angie in the Queen Vic.

The *Only Fools and Horses* episode was the one where Del Boy and Rodney inadvertently became millionaires.

The most-watched one-off event in Britain was the 1966 World Cup final when England beat West Germany 4–2 after extra time (32.3 million viewers), narrowly pipping the funeral of Diana, Princess of Wales in 1997 (32.1 million).

A few surprising TV and radio facts

In the USA in the 1930s, radio dramas were sponsored by soap manufacturers Proctor & Gamble, Colgate-Palmolive and Lever Brothers, who advertised their products during the intervals. The programmes became known as soap operas and the term stuck with the later television equivalents.

An everyday story of the people who live in a farming community doesn't sound much to get excited about, yet the BBC Radio 4 programme *The Archers* has been on the go since 1950 and is today the longest-running soap opera in any format anywhere in the world. Each 12-minute episode still attracts five million listeners.

By the age of 18 the average American child will have seen 16,000 simulated murders on television.

Disney's first-choice name for Hannah Montana (played by Miley Cyrus) was Alexis Texas, only to find that the name was already taken by a porn star.

Since the *Game of Thrones* blockbuster TV series started to air in 2011, the character names have become increasingly popular for new-born babies. Arya, Sansa, Theon and Tyrion have been welcomed into the world in numbers, and many *Thrones* babies have been named after Daenerys Stormborn of House Targaryen, Khaleesi of the Great Grass Sea, Breaker of Chains, Mother of Dragons. Fortunately for the children concerned, most parents have opted for the much shortened version of just Khaleesi.

In the finale of the 2006 series of *American Idol*, 63 million votes were cast, which was more than any elected US president had ever received. It wasn't until two years later, when Barack Obama secured the highest number of votes ever won by a presidential candidate (69.5 million), that any president received more votes than *Idol*.

In the American horror drama *The Walking Dead*, the cast holds special 'death dinners' for actors and actresses who get killed off on the show. That's a lot of death dinners.

All characters in *The Simpsons* have four fingers on each hand and four toes on each foot, although an exception is made for God, who has the odd cameo role.

The chunky-knit jumpers worn by detective Sarah Lund in the Scandi noir drama *The Killing* became something of a cult in Denmark and Britain, to the extent that the manufacturers on the Faroe Islands couldn't keep up with demand and became embroiled in legal battles over the rights of other companies to copy their styles or offer knit-your-own versions.

CELEBRITIES

Celebrities nowadays come in many guises. There are proper talented ones, like great actors and top sports people; there are ordinary people who gain vast followings because they appear on reality TV programmes like *Big Brother* and *TOWIE* (*The Only Way is Essex*); there are ones that used to be celebrities and appear on programmes like *I'm a Celebrity, Get Me Out of Here!* in the desperate hope of regaining their celebrity status by eating a kangaroo's penis; and there are celebrities who are famous just for being famous, like socialites and footballers' wives. Let's have a closer look at some of them, because that's what they're there for.

A few surprising celebrity facts

You Only Live Once is Katie Price's fourth autobiography.

Pop impresario Simon Cowell used to polish Jack Nicholson's axe when he worked as a runner during the filming of *The Shining*.

The Canadian actor James Doohan, who played Chief Engineer Scotty on *Star Trek*, killed two German snipers and took six bullets from a Bren Gun fired by a very nervous fellow Canadian soldier on D-Day.

American actor Woody Harrelson's father was a contract killer.

American sex therapist Dr Ruth was a trained sniper in the Israel Defence Forces.

British actress Helen Mirren was born Ilyena Lydia Vasilievna Mironova (her father was Russian).

Singer Adele's full name is Adele Laurie Blue Adkins.

American actor Johnny Depp suffers from coulrophobia, a fear of clowns.

When Daniel Radcliffe's parents found out he had been given the part of Harry Potter at the age of 11, they rewarded him by letting him stay up an extra half-hour to watch *Fawlty Towers*.

Legendary footballer David Beckham has over 40 tattoos and counting. They include the following:

- His wife Victoria's name in Sanskrit.
- The names of his three sons (Brooklyn, Romeo and Cruz) and one daughter (Harper).
- The Latin numeral VII, representing the number 7 shirt he wore for Manchester United.
- The number 23 – the shirt number he wore at Real Madrid and LA Galaxy.

- The number 99, to mark the year (1999) that he married Victoria Adams, and won the treble (Premier League, FA Cup and UEFA Champions League) with Manchester United.
- The words 'Let Them Hate, As Long As They Fear', which was the Roman emperor Caligula's favourite saying.
- The words 'Dream Big, Be Unrealistic' – a phrase said by the American rapper Jay-Z during a concert.
- Himself as Jesus with three cherubs, representing his sons, lifting him out of a tomb (he might have got a bit carried away with this one).

Highest-earning dead celebrities

Just because you're a dead celebrity, it doesn't mean you can't go on raking it in. Here are the annual earnings of some very famous dead ones:

Michael Jackson:	$115million
Elvis Presley:	$55 million
Charles M. Schulz (the *Peanuts* cartoonist):	$40 million
Bob Marley:	$21 million
Elizabeth Taylor:	$20 million

FOOD AND DRINK

Apart from being quite necessary to stay alive and healthy, food and drink are increasingly important from a social point of view in a society where we want for very little, so we should know as much about them as we can.

A few surprising food and drink facts

Starbucks coffee shops offer 80,000 different drinks combinations.

Russia didn't classify beer as alcohol until 2011, having previously considered it to be a soft drink (which, compared to their vodka, it probably is).

A lethal dose of chocolate for a human being is about 40 regular bars of Cadbury's Dairy Milk.

The steak dish Tournedos Rossini wasn't just named after the Italian composer; it was likely invented by him after he gave up composing to indulge his other passion of gourmet cooking, having been an excellent amateur chef his whole life.

When the first drive-through McDonald's opened in Kuwait, the queue caused a tailback seven miles long.

Candied grasshoppers are a popular snack in Japan. So is everything else.

Knowledge is knowing that a tomato is a fruit. Wisdom is not putting it in a fruit salad.

There is no Guinness World Record for drinking the most Guinness, or for any other alcohol-drinking achievements. Probably just as well.

HP Sauce is so called because its brown-sauce recipe was reportedly used in the restaurant at the Houses of Parliament at the turn of the twentieth century.

Every year four million cats are eaten in Asia.

It takes around 700 grapes to make a bottle of wine.

Historians argue over the veracity of the story behind the naming of sirloin steak, and over which monarch or monarchs were involved (favourites include Henry VIII, Elizabeth I and James I), but it is widely touted to this day that one or more of those monarchs used to declare the evening's feast to be open by knighting the side of beef that had been brought before them with the words: 'Arise, Sir Loin.' Historians of a more etymological bent argue that the name derives from the Old French word *surloigne*, meaning 'above the loin', but where's the fun in that?

Tiramisu means 'pick me up' in Italian.

If you've ever wondered what the different names for pasta mean, you could probably work some of them out just by looking at them. If you can't be bothered, here are some of the main ones translated from Italian into English:

Spaghetti = thin strings
Vermicelli = little worms
Linguine = little tongues
Cannelloni = large reeds
Gemelli = twins
Penne = quill pens

Conchiglie = shells
Farfalle = bowties or butterflies (they're the same word in Italian)
Fiori = flowers
Orecchiette = little ears
Tortellini = little pies

According to *Vegan Life* magazine, the number of vegans in the UK alone has increased by 360 per cent in the last ten years and there are now over half a million people in the UK following the plant-based diet that avoids all foods that come from animals.

A greater awareness of gluten intolerance and an increasing number of sufferers worldwide have brought about demand for gluten-free food that does not taste like a brick. Gluten is the general term for the proteins found in wheat and related grains, including barley, rye and oats. It is the glue (from the Latin *gluten*) that holds food together, but it also happens to be the glue that makes wheat-related foods tasty, hence the need for food scientists to find an alternative glue that tastes like the real stuff.

Avocados are so prized nowadays that after a poor harvest in the first half of 2016, over 14,000 were stolen from orchards around New Zealand to be sold on the black market.

FASHION

Even if you're a dedicated follower of fashion, here are a few less obvious things you may not have known:

Denim jeans are not as American as you might think. When Levi Strauss wanted a strong enough fabric to make clothing for the gold-diggers, cowboys and railroad builders of the Wild West, he turned to a family in the French city of Nîmes, who had developed a durable fabric known as *serge*. Strauss imported as much *serge de Nîmes* as he could get his hands on and it wasn't long before *de Nîmes* became denim in American English – and the rest is clothing history.

In North Korea jeans and piercings are banned on the grounds that they are too capitalist, and people have to choose from a state-sanctioned list of haircuts. If men really want to curry favour, they can go for the roadkill-perched-on-top-of-the-head style sported by dictator Kim Jong-un.

One third of the world's socks are made in a township called Datang in Zhuji, China. In one year, they produce the equivalent of two pairs of socks for every person in the world.

The bikini was so called because its French creator thought it would create a shock as big as the atomic bombs tested by the Americans on Bikini Atoll in the Pacific after the Second World War.

It is considered offensive to show the sole of your shoe in Arab culture because it is always in contact with the dirty ground.

The reason we have decorative buttons on jacket sleeves came about because Napoleon got fed up with his soldiers wiping their runny noses on their sleeves.

Neckties are the most common Father's Day gift worldwide.

The Lacoste clothing brand was named after French tennis player René Lacoste, who won seven Grand Slam tournaments in the 1920s and who was nicknamed '*le crocodile*' by his followers. The crocodile of Lacoste was only the second ever brand logo to appear on an item of clothing, the first having been the iconic diving girl of swimwear company Jantzen.

Panama hats are not made in Panama, and they never have been. They have always been made in Ecuador, but in the nineteenth century there wasn't much passing trade in Ecuador so the manufacturers there took their hats up to Panama, where there was a huge amount of passing trade. Wherever the proud owners of the hats went in the world thereafter, people asked them where they got their lovely new hats. 'Panama,' they said.

SOCIAL MEDIA AND ONLINE SHOPPING

It is now perfectly possible to manage your life and your relationships electronically, including the opportunity to have anything and everything delivered to your front door within a day or two of ordering it online. Let's have a look at the options that allow us to live the life of a twenty-first-century recluse if we so choose:

The Microsoft Corporation founded by Bill Gates in 1975 remains the world's largest supplier of personal computers, software and electronics, including its flagship Microsoft Office suite and Xbox game consoles.

Since Amazon was founded by Jeff Bezos in 1994 as an online bookstore, it has grown to provide just about anything to its some 250 million active users. It is currently the largest internet-based retailer in the USA.

Around 12 new books are added to Amazon every hour of every day. This book is one of about four million now available on Amazon, so you did very well to find it if that's where you bought it, and I'm very pleased you did.

Even Amazon is dwarfed by the world's largest e-commerce company Alibaba, which sells up to $300 billion of goods worldwide out of China every year. On 31 March 2016, Alibaba also became the world's largest overall retailer, knocking Walmart into second place.

The Apple company founded by Steve Jobs, Steve Wozniak and Ronald Wayne in 1976 probably remains the coolest thing in technology worldwide, providing everything from computers, laptops, tablets and phones to music, video, apps and gadgets to meet your every need. It is the world's most valuable brand (worth around $120 billion) and even the address of its headquarters is pretty cool:

> Apple Campus, 1 Infinite Loop, Cupertino, California.

Every Apple ad displays the time on the iPhone, iPad or Mac as 9:41. It used to be 9:42, which was the time of the day Steve Jobs unveiled the first iPhone in 2007, 42 minutes into his keynote presentation. In 2010, with the release of the first iPad, they decided to move the ad time back a minute, presumably because they'd got a bit quicker with their launch presentations.

The terms and conditions which none of us read when we accept updates to the iTunes app include the condition that we will not use the app for 'the development, design, manufacture or production of nuclear, missiles, or chemical or biological weapons'.

French-born American entrepreneur Pierre Omidyar was responsible for the launch of the eBay consumer-to-consumer and business-to-consumer auction site, which has since expanded to provide 'Buy It Now' shopping alongside online auctions in over 30 countries. Its revenue in 2015 was $8.59 billion. Who says the French don't have a word for entrepreneur?

With another five to eight hours' worth being added every minute, it would already take over a thousand years to watch all the videos on YouTube, so you need to be picky if you don't think you'll live that long or if you have other stuff to do.

American student Mark Zuckerberg launched Facebook on his college campus at Harvard in 2004. Within three years it had been made available to everyone in the world over the age of 13 with a valid email address. Now it has over 1.6 billion active users. The story behind the creation of Facebook has been captured in the 2010 film *The Social Network* starring Jesse Eisenberg (as Zuckerberg), Andrew Garfield and Justin Timberlake.

The first ever tweet on Twitter was sent by the network's co-founder Jack Dorsey in 2006. It read: 'just setting up my twttr'. Now about 500 million tweets are posted each day by around 300 million users, and the words posted in Twitter feeds each day would fill a ten-million-page book.

Online gambling sites allow you to speculate on just about anything, including poker, horse racing and the chances of it being a white Christmas. All you need to do is hand over money electronically – most or all of which you are going to lose, so it's not that different to popping down the betting shop, really.

For the twelve months up to September 2015, the Gambling Commission reported that online gambling in the UK accounted for around a third of the county's £12.6 billion gambling industry.

In the year ending 31 March 2016, the UK's National Lottery recorded receipts of £7,595 million, which it disposed of as follows:

1. £4,198 million paid out in prizes
2. £1,901 million allocated to National Lottery projects
3. £911 million paid to the government in Lottery Duty
4. £333 million paid out in retailers' commission

Of the £1,901 million allocated to projects, 40 per cent went into health, education, environment and charitable causes. The remaining 60 per cent was divided equally between causes relating to sport, the arts and heritage.

Internet dating sites have become big business for every flavour and age of would-be dater and have resulted in a lot of relationships and marriages that could never otherwise have happened, but beware: the founder of match. com, Gary Kremen, lost his girlfriend to a man she found on match.com

THINGS THAT DO YOUR HEAD IN

INTRODUCTION

There are some things in life that are just a bit difficult to understand, like science and technology, maths and politics. It's fine when clever clogs get together and talk to each other about these things, say at a conference or a seminar, but sometimes they turn up at parties alongside ordinary people. You can't even see them coming because they don't always wear their white coats or anoraks and this allows them to blend in seamlessly.

In this chapter I'm going to give you some random things to say to clever people so that they think you're quite clever too, but never use more than one of these things at a time and always say you have to go the toilet now before they have a chance to say something back to you. This will have the added advantage of making you look mysterious.

SCIENCE

Sometimes scientists discover stuff that helps us understand more about life, the world we live in and the known universe, which is all very well, but sometimes they discover stuff which can make a big difference to the quality of human existence, which is why we should all encourage them to carry on the good work. Polish-born French chemist and physicist Marie Curie couldn't have known that her work on the discovery of radium would lead to improved cancer treatment for millions of people. British scientist Michael Faraday could hardly have guessed that his work on electromagnetism and electrochemistry would one day allow the powering up of everything from a light bulb to heavy industrial machinery. Here are some interesting facts about scientists before we look at the kind of work they do:

The Italian Leonardo da Vinci wasn't just the guy who painted the *Mona Lisa* and *The Last Supper*, he was probably the most versatile guy who ever lived. He was an artist, inventor, scientist, mathematician, engineer, writer and musician. He could even write with one hand and draw with the other at the same time, although you needed a mirror to see what he had written because he wrote backwards. My one criticism of da Vinci, in fact, is that I can't understand his more elaborate scientific treatises without a mirror.

English physicist and mathematician Isaac Newton didn't just discover that apples fell from trees through the force of gravity, he also came up with the laws of motion, the first practical telescope and the first coins to be designed and produced with anti-counterfeit measures (while he was Warden of the Royal Mint).

STUFF AND NONSENSE

Laws of motion explained

I thought it might help to offer a practical example of Isaac Newton's laws of motion, just in case a scientist asks you what you think of them in order to find out if you're clever enough to continue talking to:

1. If you don't kick a dead badger, it won't go anywhere. If you don't kick a dead badger on a travelator (at an airport, say), its velocity won't change (until it reaches the end of the travelator, at least).
2. If you kick a dead badger, it will change its velocity and probably its direction. The harder you kick it, the more it will fly off in some direction or other.
3. If you kick a rock disguised as a dead badger, it will hurt your foot, because the rock will react by exerting equal pressure right back at you.

In 1903, Marie Curie became the first woman to win a Nobel Prize, and in 1911 she became the only person to have won the prize for two different sciences (Physics and Chemistry). Her good work didn't stop with her either, because her daughter Irène also went on to win the Nobel Prize for Chemistry in 1936.

The German-born theoretical physicist Albert Einstein is best known for his general theory of relativity, one of the pillars of modern physics, and for producing the most famous equation known to man: $E = mc^2$, or energy equals mass times the speed of light squared. The reason for it not being $E = ms^2$ is that he used *celeritas*, the Latin word for speed (or 'swiftness'), because scientists just do stuff like that sometimes.

Albert Einstein was so in awe of Michael Faraday's achievements that he kept a picture of him on his study wall.

English naturalist Charles Darwin changed the way humans viewed themselves forever. His work on evolution and natural selection challenged the long-held view that all life was as it was for the sole reason that that is how it had been created by whatever god or gods people believed in.

French microbiologist Louis Pasteur made our milk safe to drink, and apparently quite tasty (I don't like milk, so I can offer no personal view on the subject), by the method still known as pasteurisation in his honour. He also produced the first vaccine against rabies and countless other advances in the treatment of disease.

The Swedish polymath responsible for bequeathing the Nobel Prize to the world was Alfred Nobel. Fluent in several languages and a writer of poetry and drama, he was also a chemist, inventor and very successful businessman, having 355 patents to his name, one of which was for the invention of dynamite. Notwithstanding the dynamite thing (which he meant to be used for industrial purposes only), he was particularly keen on world peace, which is why there is a Peace Prize alongside those for Chemistry, Physics, Medicine and Literature.

British biochemist **Dorothy Hodgkin** is known as the founder of protein crystallography, which means in English that she helped discover the structure of proteins, including those relating to penicillin and vitamin B_{12}, which won her the Nobel Prize for Chemistry in 1964. She was a lecturer and therefore a faculty member at Oxford University for much of the time that she carried out her research there, but she wasn't allowed to go to research meetings because she was a woman. She *was* allowed to teach a pupil by the name of Margaret Roberts (later Thatcher), who went on to attend (and chair) as many meetings as she liked as prime minister of the United Kingdom.

Physics

Matter is what matters to a physicist, and so is energy. When energy and matter get together, they get really excited, and so do physicists. Here is some stuff that really matters:

You can't make yourself cold, because cold is just the natural state of things unless and until you wobble some of your molecules. If you want to impress a physicist at a party, just say: 'My goodness, I seem to have reverted to my natural state.' If you're in luck, the physicist may offer to wobble your molecules somewhat.

If you want to lose weight, move to Mars, where you will weigh less than half as much as you do on earth.

If the empty space in atoms could be removed, the entire human race could shrink down to the size of a sugar cube, but the sugar cube would weigh ten times more than all humans currently alive. We are literally a waste of space.

There are more atoms in a teaspoonful of water than there are teaspoonfuls of water in the Atlantic Ocean.

'Albert Einstein' is an anagram of 'ten elite brains'.

The foam that exists in whipped cream, bubble baths and beer is 95 per cent gas and 5 per cent liquid. If a physicist ever asks you if you want to go out and get a bit gassed, be very afraid.

Sound travels more quickly through water. If you don't believe me, listen to the notes you make when you play a guitar and then play that same guitar underwater and see if you can tell the difference. If you just tried this experiment using an electric guitar, I'm afraid you won't be moving on with us into the Chemistry section of this chapter.

Chemistry

Chemistry may be more elementary than Physics, but it still matters and it's still difficult. Here is some elementary stuff to get you going:

Everything in the universe is made from atoms that join together to make molecules that join together to make one of the 118 elements (of which 94 are naturally occurring, and 24 are synthetic) that are the basis of everything that exists.

Because some elements are well hard (like titanium), some are proper runny (like mercury) and some are a real gas (like helium), it can be difficult to keep track of their various properties and relationships with one another. Thankfully, a helpful Russian chemist called Dmitri Mendeleev organised them into a useful structure called the Periodic Table (because of the repeating, or periodical, nature of the properties of each element).

Some elements have been known about for thousands of years (like gold, silver and carbon); others have only recently been discovered (like ununoctium and the most recent one of all, ununseptium). It is a general rule of thumb in science that the most recent discoveries have to have the most stupid names, at least while they're waiting for their longer-term names to be established – it is proposed that ununoctium should become oganesson (after the Russian scientist involved in the discovery) and that ununseptium should become tennessine (after the state of Tennessee, where much of the research took place).

If you want to make some ununoctium at home, just fuse a bit of lead with some krypton (but don't let Superman catch you doing it, because he might think you're working with Lex Luther).

Once atoms and molecules get together, they become things that we know about, like H_2O (water) and CO_2 (carbon dioxide). If you get stuck with a chemist at a party, always speak in symbols wherever possible. It helps to break the frozen H_2O and they will fall about the floor laughing.

You don't even need to use chemical symbols to be hilarious at a dinner party; you just need to know the elements within the compounds on the dining-room table. For example, you can ask someone to please pass you sodium and chloride in equal measure once you understand the constituent parts of table salt. You'll be the talk of the dinner-party circuit with this one, I promise you.

It's the 2 in CO_2, the di in dioxide, that keeps us alive. Just CO, or carbon monoxide, is not nearly as good for us. It's not much use for the planet either, which is why car exhaust fumes are a bit of an issue.

The core of the earth is largely made of iron, the air is mostly made of nitrogen (only 21 per cent is oxygen) and all living things have their base in carbon, so another great line to impress a chemist at a party is: 'I'm feeling a bit faint. In fact, I'm not at all sure that my carbon is getting enough nitrogen standing here on this lump of iron.' Tears should be running down the chemist's face by now.

The most expensive element on earth is californium. If you have to ask the price of a piece of californium jewellery, you can't afford it. In fact, it would cost about a million times more than the equivalent piece of gold jewellery, but there's no such thing as californium jewellery anyway because californium is used to fire up a nuclear reactor and nobody wants one of those babies on their finger.

Biology and medicine

We owe much of our understanding of living things, including human living things, to great biologists like Charles Darwin and his contemporary Alfred Russel Wallace; Carl Linnaeus, the father of taxonomy (the naming and classifying of things); Gregor Mendel, the first man clever enough to understand genetics – I assume he got his brains from his father; Francis Crick and James Watson, the discoverers of the structure of DNA; and Keith Campbell and Ian Wilmut, who controversially cloned a sheep called Dolly. Here are some biological and medical germs of thought to make you sound like you know what you're talking about:

Biologists reckon that most component parts of the human body replace themselves on such a regular basis that your body is likely to always be on average less than ten years old. If you sometimes don't feel quite like your old self, you're probably right. If you've been in a relationship for a while, the person you're sleeping with isn't quite the same person you first met. Watch your back.

The average human gets through 900 skins in a lifetime. I think a new skin is something to be celebrated, and just think how many 'Happy Skinday' presents we could get (about one every 30 days).

Two of the most difficult things to change going through life are your DNA code and your Facebook history. Your DNA code helpfully allows you to replace your atoms on a like-for-like basis, and your Facebook history less than helpfully forms a permanent record of your personality when you're drunk.

The Hippocratic Oath to uphold ethical standards of medicine is still taken by many graduating physicians today, but dates back to the fifth century BCE when students of the Greek physician Hippocrates were required to swear by it. There are variations on the theme today, like the Osteopathic Oath, but make no bones about it, the Hippocratic Oath is still very much the original.

If someone prods one of our three middle toes while our eyes are shut, it is apparently difficult to know which toe was prodded. (I had this done to me a few times and I ended up with a 50/50 record of getting it right or wrong.)

Adult skeletons have 206 bones, without which we would just flop shapelessly about, like teenagers on a Saturday night in Ibiza. We actually start life with 270 bones, but by the time we reach adulthood a number of them have fused together. One of the reasons we start off with more is that it's easier to wriggle out through the birth canal with a few extra joints.

Most of our joints only move in one direction, like the hinges of a door, but our ball-and-socket hip and shoulder joints allow much more dynamic movement. Without our ball-and-socket joints, we would be much less adept at sport and our dancing repertoire would be limited to the hokey cokey.

Most things that exist on earth are microorganisms. They are all too little to see with the naked eye and most of them are harmless to us, but some of them are the single-cell bacteria that cause diseases and some are viruses which need to reproduce by using the cells of other living things, like human beings. The worst virus known to mankind is, of course, man flu, which hurts even more than childbirth. If a woman was to catch man flu, her life would be over in a matter of minutes, that's how bad it is.

There are seven things we need to do to survive as 'living things': breathe, move, grow, eat, excrete, react and reproduce. Reproduction is the only one that doesn't have to be done on an individual basis, but it does require enough of us to have a bash to ensure the survival of the species.

In 1974, Dr Henry Heimlich introduced his technique of upward thrusts of a fist below the chest for dislodging food or objects stuck in people's throats. It is credited with saving thousands of lives since then, although he never actually used the technique himself as a practising doctor. One evening in May 2016, however, at the ripe old age of 96, he noticed that the elderly female resident sitting next to him at the dinner table in their retirement home in Cincinnati, Ohio, was choking. With all eyes upon him, he successfully delivered his own Heimlich manoeuvre to dislodge a piece of hamburger and thereby save his dining companion's life. If you ask me, he deserved that moment.

MATHEMATICS

Ever since Pythagoras turned Maths into a subject to be revered in Ancient Greece, and Archimedes worked out how many grains of sand would fill the universe, the world has been divided into people who like Maths and people who are afraid of Maths. Here is some stuff to make you sound clever on the subject, but don't worry about this one too much as people who like Maths rarely go to parties anyway:

Because geometry is about shapes, lines and angles, it is of use to architects and engineers (triangles are particularly strong, apparently). Even builders love geometrical shapes, because cuboids fit together a treat, although they insist on calling their cuboids 'bricks' for reasons not understood by people who love Maths.

Pythagoras thought that everything could be broken down into numbers, including astronomy, nature and music. If someone ever tells you that they're a big fan of Pythagoras, RUN!

The Fibonacci Sequence is a series of numbers where you calculate the next number by adding together the previous two numbers (1, 1, 2, 3, 5, 8, 13, etc.). That appears quite dull until you realise that it occurs naturally in things which spiral a lot, like sunflower seeds and the arrangement of a pine cone. Coincidence, or what?

The atoms in a diamond are arranged as a pattern of interlocking tetrahedrons and that's what makes them one of the world's hardest substances. Whenever two geometry graduates get married, their vows include the words: 'With this pattern of interlocking tetrahedron, I thee wed.'

Algebra is cool if you prefer letters to numbers because it has equations like $F = mg$, which was Isaac Newton's way of saying that the force of gravity is equal to the mass of a falling object times its gravitational acceleration. This law of universal gravitation can be useful to know if you find yourself falling off a wall and you want to know how much it's going to hurt when you make impact with the pavement below (unless, of course, you're falling off a wall in the USA, in which case you'll want to know how much it's going to hurt when you make impact with the sidewalk below).

A pizza that has a radius of 'Z' and a height of 'A' has a volume of Pi x Z x Z x A.

The French word for pie chart is Camembert.

Statistics are great for predicting the future based on what happened in the past. Compare the weather patterns in Key West, Florida and in the Russian province of Siberia during the month of May for the last 20 years and your findings will show that being in Key West during the month of May next year will, in all probability, feel warmer than being in Siberia at the same time.

I thought about putting in a cool fact about Calculus, but I didn't want to go off on a tangent.

TECHNOLOGY

It's easy to take technology for granted, especially if you're under the age of 40 and computers, laptops, tablets and mobile phones are all perfectly intuitive to you. We should not, however, forget that we got to where we are today thanks to the genius of technology wizards like Alan Turing (invented the computer), Tim Berners-Lee (invented the World Wide Web), Bill Gates (responsible for the personal computer revolution), Steve Jobs (responsible for the microcomputer revolution), Mark Zuckerberg (invented Facebook) and Elon Musk (the guy at the forefront of electric car and space transportation technology). Here are some cool facts about those wizards and about the technology they brought to the world:

English mathematician Alan Turing invented the computer even before he set about breaking the German Enigma code during the Second World War. Breaking the code is said to have shortened the war by several years and thereby saved millions of lives.

English computer scientist Tim Berners-Lee was a keen trainspotter as a child and picked up a basic knowledge of electronics through tinkering with his model railway. It was, of course, only a small jump from tinkering with a model railway to inventing the World Wide Web.

Steve Jobs took a salary of $1 per annum as CEO of Apple Inc. from 1997 to 2011, but his 5.5 million shares in his own company rose from $3.19 to $365 over that same period. Do the maths.

South African-born American-Canadian business magnate Elon Musk is nothing if not ambitious. One of his stated objectives is to colonise Mars, and if his space freight and plug-in electric car ventures are anything to go by, he might just succeed. He already supplies the International Space Station with cargo runs akin to supermarket home deliveries back on earth.

The jigsaws, board games (like ludo, Cluedo, snakes and ladders and Monopoly) and hands-on games (like Bucking Bronco, Jenga and Twister) of yesteryear have been superseded by computer games like Crypt of the NecroDancer, The Witcher, Grim Fandango Remastered, Grand Theft Auto, Candy Crush Saga and Minecraft. This may or may not be progress. Discuss.

The best-selling video game in history is Tetris, with sales of approximately 500 million since its release in 1984. This easily outstrips the best-selling board game of the last century, Monopoly, which has achieved sales of approximately 250 million. Chess, draughts (or checkers) and backgammon have been around for thousands of years and have probably, therefore, enjoyed more sales than even Tetris, but it didn't occur to anyone to keep the sales figures way back when.

Today's mobile phones have more computing power than the computers used in the Apollo 11 mission – to land humans on the moon – in 1969.

Today, the people on earth take more photos in two minutes than they did in the whole of the nineteenth century.

Buzz Aldrin, the second man to walk on the moon in 1969 (20 minutes after Neil Armstrong), had already taken the first space selfie during a spacewalk in 1966, with planet earth as his backdrop.

More people die while taking selfies than from shark attacks. Here are some of the ways in which they have met their untimely deaths while trying to capture that special moment:

1. Shooting themselves while pointing a loaded gun at their heads (I can only assume they meant to press the phone-camera button with the other hand and got mixed up in the heat of the moment).
2. Being hit by moving trains (this is an especially popular way to die in India).
3. Coming into contact with live overhead wires while posing on top of trains (you wouldn't believe how often this has happened).
4. Drowning after falling into water, usually from high rocks, bridges or dams.
5. Falling off the top of high buildings.
6. Pulling a pin from a hand-grenade (if it weren't for the selfie, it would have been difficult to establish the cause of death from what was left of these particular idiots).
7. Being gored by the oncoming bull in the backdrop during an annual bull-running festival (the moment of imminent death was perfectly captured for the coroner, whose verdict on the cause of death was 'sheer f*****g stupidity').

8. Losing control of the light aircraft the selfie-taker was piloting. Really.
9. Falling into a volcano, presumably while saying cheeeeeeeeeeeeese!

When Montenegro gained independence from Yugoslavia, its domain suffix went from being .yu to .me.

An alternative used for LOL in Thai text speak is 555, because 5 in Thai is pronounced 'ha'.

Twenty-first-century vocabulary

If you're going to live in the twenty-first century, you really should learn the language required to do so successfully. Here are a few essential words to get you started:

Friendorphobia is the fear of forgetting your passwords.

Cyberchondria is the term used to describe hypochondria brought about or exaggerated by convincing yourself that you have diseases or illnesses that you found by trawling through the countless online medical sites that have sprung up to explain every symptom known to mankind. The most common symptom of cyberchondria is unnecessary anxiety. If you don't believe me, look it up.

Egosurfing is the act of searching the web to see what turns up under your own name.

Googleganger is the name given to the people who turn up with the same name as you when you egosurf. If I google myself, I turn up alongside the entry for the Ray Hamilton who played tight end for the Washington Redskins, the extensive album discography of the Ray Hamilton Orchestra (including the must-have *It Takes Two to Cha Cha*) and the entry for the Ray Hamilton who was sprung from prison by fellow gang members Bonnie and Clyde just before they themselves were gunned down. See what fun you can have egosurfing? Go on, you know you want to meet your own Googlegangers.

An internet meme is an image, video, hashtag, etc. that is posted online and passed on through social media. It often leads to the fad in question being copied, like the art of planking, which involves lying face-down to have your photo taken in a public space. Other popular photo poses include tea-potting and dressing animals up in human clothing, and video dance crazes include the 'Harlem Shake' and the 'Gangnam Style' horse riding routine.

   The word 'meme' was initially coined by author Richard Dawkins, in his 1976 book *The Selfish Gene*, to describe the phenomenon of transmitting cultural ideas or practices by means of mimicking.

STUFF AND NONSENSE

Smiley face and beyond

In 2015, for the first time ever, the Oxford Dictionaries Word of the Year was not even a word. It was the pictograph, or emoji, known as 'Face with Tears of Joy'. The original emoji, the smiley face, was commissioned in 1963 by a Massachusetts insurance company to boost the morale of its employees, and it remains popular around the world, but different cultures embrace certain emojis more enthusiastically than others, with text messages in the UK, for example, using the winky face at twice the average global rate. A recent survey by an online dating site claims that people who use emojis get more sex than those who don't. If you're not getting enough, maybe you should think about getting that winky out a bit more.

POLITICS

Don't worry, I'm not going to go all party politics on us here, but there are some things we need to know about politics because other people do have an annoying tendency to talk to us about this most difficult of subjects:

When Edinburgh Zoo took delivery of two giant pandas, Tian Tian and Yang Guang, in 2011, it became a standing joke that there were twice as many pandas as Conservative MPs in Scotland, but Conservative

MPs made something of a comeback in the Scottish Parliament election of 2016, winning 15 seats. All is not lost, though, because Tian Tian was artificially inseminated the same week as the election was held and there remains a glimmer of hope that giant pandas will once more become the less endangered of the two species. There has even been talk of releasing some of the Conservative MPs back into the wild.

Saudi women have the right to vote but not the right to drive to the polling stations.

The former leader of the UK's Liberal Democrat party, Nick Clegg, had to do community service after setting fire to a rare cactus collection on a school trip.

India is the world's largest democracy, with almost a billion registered voters.

It is not uncommon for over 50 per cent of the votes cast in a British general election to be for losing candidates, and to therefore count for nothing in a first-past-the-post system.

Bolivia has the highest turnover of governments in the world, with around 200 since gaining independence from Spain in 1825.

In 1984, ex-movie actor Ronald Reagan got the most electoral college votes of any US presidential candidate in history. In 1964 he had been turned down for the role of US president in a movie because he wasn't considered to have 'the presidential look'.

David 'Screaming Lord Sutch', as leader of the Official Monster Raving Loony Party from 1983 to 1999, holds the record as Britain's longest-serving party leader.

William Pulteney, the first Earl of Bath, was the least successful British prime minister in history, having given up on his attempts to form a Cabinet in 1746 after just two days (he couldn't persuade enough MPs to work with him). The phrase 'having an Early Bath' is still very much in use today.

In local elections held in Antigua in 2015, the campaign posters for the party that promised improved education contained the slogan 'Leaning for All'.

In 1965 Hawaiian politician Patsy Takemoto Mink became the first Asian-American woman and the first woman of colour to be elected to Congress. In 2002 she became the first deceased woman of colour to be elected to Congress, having died just after the primary election and therefore too late to have her name removed from the general election ballot. A month after her state funeral, Congress re-elected her posthumously as a mark of respect until her seat could be filled.

In 2010 the Italian government had a fleet of 629,000 official cars – ten times more than the US government. Around 628,000 of them were probably used to take then-prime minister Silvio Berlusconi's 'girlfriends' to the many parties he threw to unwind after a hard day's prime ministering.

The general election in North Korea in 1962 recorded a 100 per cent turnout of voters and a 100 per cent vote for the Workers' Party of Korea, a quite astonishing achievement and a record that is unlikely to ever be beaten. The turnout of voters in the 2014 election plummeted to 99.97 per cent, but maintained a 100 per cent vote for the sole party up for election, the Democratic Front for the Reunification of the Fatherland, which has now subsumed the Workers' Party of Korea.

In 1927, Charles D. B. King was elected President of Liberia with a majority that was 15 times the size of the total electorate. He resigned before the next election before he could be impeached for rigging the 1927 results.

In the 2002 general election in Iraq, Saddam Hussein chose 'I Will Always Love You' as his campaign song. The Dolly Parton song made famous by Whitney Houston in the 1992 film *The Bodyguard* was sung on this occasion by a Syrian pop star and was played from morning to night all over Iraq. It worked in his favour, because Saddam Hussein received 100 per cent of the vote that year and we will just never know whether he would have been re-elected if he had chosen a less popular song to campaign with.

BANKING

Bankers today are right up there with politicians as the most-lambasted members of society, but it wasn't always so, and they remain necessary to oil the machinery of government, industry and personal finance, whether we like it or not. Here are some facts to use if you get stuck at a party with a banker who won't stop trying to sell you something you don't really need:

The earliest banks were to be found in Ancient Mesopotamia, where grain merchants would pay to store their grain in temples (the cool atmosphere within temples was ideal for food storage) and make deposits and withdrawals as necessary. Transactions were carried out by weight and some of the terminology has stuck even through to the present day, e.g. the British pound.

Tens of thousands of damaged bank notes (many of which have been chewed by dogs) are replaced each year at no cost to the bearer. The Bank of England used to incinerate them to support its central heating system, but it now takes the more environmentally friendly action of shredding them. At one Bank of England site, between 1988 and 1992, workers stole over half a million pounds destined for disposal by walking out with them in their underwear.

Scottish and Northern Irish notes are not technically legal tender, which means that no one is legally obliged to accept them as payment for debts, goods or services, but they are fine to use because the total value of the notes in circulation is guaranteed by internal Bank of England banknotes called Titans (A4 size, worth £100 million) and Giants (A5 size, worth £1 million). Conversely, Bank of England notes are only legal tender in England and Wales, not in Scotland or Northern Ireland. The entire banking system turns a blind eye to these weird anomalies, and Danske Bank in Northern Ireland doesn't even pretend it's not Danish while carrying on business there, so just spend whatever notes you have wherever you are in the UK, even if they're issued by the far-off Hong Kong and Shanghai Banking Corporation (HSBC).

The word 'bankrupt' comes from the Italian *banca rotta*, meaning the 'broken bench' of a moneylender who could no longer finance his own business. Famous people who have gone *banca rotta* include Abraham Lincoln, Oscar Wilde, Walt Disney, Mike Tyson and Lady Gaga. Mike Tyson's debts at the time of his bankruptcy included £264,000 for an unpaid birthday party and £5,000 in care for his pet tigers. The man is clearly an idiot and you can tell him I said so the next time you see him.

In 2011 a man in North Carolina held up a bank for $1 and then waited to be arrested so that he could gain access to the free healthcare available to prison inmates.

Winston Churchill is the face on the reverse of the new Bank of England £5 note. The note, 15 per cent smaller than its predecessor, is the first of a set of more durable plastic notes which will last longer than paper notes and be more difficult to counterfeit. It will be followed in 2017 by a new £10 note featuring English writer Jane Austen, and in 2020 by the new £20 note featuring (as we have already noted in the chapter 'A Bit of Culture') English painter J. M. W. Turner.

The 'Bank of Mum and Dad' now loans about £5 billion every year in the UK alone, making it the tenth-biggest mortgage lender in the country.

TO BOLDLY GO...

INTRODUCTION

If you don't leave this chapter feeling small and insignificant, I'll know that you haven't read it properly. Our entire planet is less than a pinhead in terms of the overall size of the universe, and the human race is of no consequence whatsoever when set in the context of such magnitude. When our life-giving sun finally burns itself out, which it undoubtedly will, because all stars do, the human race will perish (if it hasn't already) and the universe won't even notice. But at least the sun has enough hydrogen to fuel itself for another five billion years so we might as well enjoy ourselves while we can, I suppose. Having said that, the sun only had ten billion years to burn in the first place, and where have the last five billion years gone?

THE UNIVERSE

Let us start with the biggest thing that we know of – the known universe (although the known universe is by its very nature smaller than the known universe plus the unknown universe, which is still probably just one universe alongside a number of universes that we don't know about yet). The known universe alone contains so many stars, galaxies, black holes, planets, comets and meteors that there's almost no point in trying to get our tiny little human minds around its utter vastness. But let's give it a go anyway.

Stars

Stars are huge balls of plasma (like a gas, but with charged particles) that give off enormous energy, heat and light. Our nearest star is the sun, which is why we exist within a 'solar system', but our sun is only one of around 200 billion stars in our one single galaxy, which in turn is really small in terms of the overall universe. In fact, there are around ten times as many stars in the known universe as there are grains of sand on earth. Are you feeling insignificant yet?

Galaxies

A galaxy is a group of millions or billions of stars, which hold themselves together by mutual gravity and are isolated from other such galaxies by vast amounts of empty space. Our galaxy is the Milky Way, but it is only one of around 80 billion galaxies. If you've ever wondered what your full postal address would be if other as-yet-undiscovered planets started to communicate with us on earth, it would be something like this:

Ms K. G. Eccles
3 Gryffe Crescent
Comber
East Sussex
TN20 6XY
United Kingdom
Planet Earth
Solar System
Milky Way Galaxy
Known Universe

Planets

Planets are rocky or gaseous objects that orbit a star (and that aren't a satellite of another object, like our moon). Luckily enough for us, they are big enough to sweep away smaller objects that come into their largely circular orbits. As far as we know, planet earth is the only one that supports life, but for all we know there might be others orbiting some far-away stars in some other galaxies. If there is, the life forms that exist there are pretty unlikely to look like anything on earth – although I do remember thinking that the first time I saw a giraffe, so never say never.

Black holes

Black holes are ex-stars that have collapsed in on themselves when gravity just became too much for them. The old star ends up surrounded by an area known as the event horizon and it is now virtually cut off from the rest of the universe. It is called an event horizon because if an event happens inside it, that event is never going to be observable from outside the black hole. Stuff can get sucked into a black hole, including light particles, but nothing, not even light, is coming back out.

Meteors, meteoroids and meteorites

A meteor is the light phenomenon we call a 'shooting star', which occurs when a meteoroid (a rock from a comet or asteroid) enters a planet's atmosphere and burns up. If it's big enough, it doesn't completely vaporise and the remains, known as a meteorite, will smash into the planet before burning out, which is probably what wiped out the dinosaurs on planet earth.

Asteroids and comets

An asteroid is an inactive, rocky body that orbits a star. A comet is a sometimes-active ball of ice, dust and gas, with a coma (a fuzzy halo of light) and often a tail of space debris.

STUFF AND NONSENSE

Halley's comet

The most famous comet visible from earth is Halley's comet, which has appeared every 75 or 76 years since at least as far back as 240 BCE. It is named after English astronomer Edmond Halley, who, in 1705, was the first person to determine how often it appeared in our skies. The last time it appeared, in 1986, astronomers were able to have a good look at it for the first time, because pictures were sent back to earth from a number of space probes sent into orbit for that very purpose. They found it to be more dust than ice, but see what you think for yourself if you're still around in 2061. Its most historical appearance was in 1066, which is why a representation of it was woven into the famous Bayeux Tapestry, which depicts the events leading up to and culminating in the Battle of Hastings.

THE SOLAR SYSTEM

A planetary system consists of a star and everything that orbits around it, including its planets, dwarf planets, asteroids, moons, comets and meteoroids (in other words, all of its 'natural satellites'). The planetary system we live in, which we call the solar system, has nearly 200 moons and used to have nine planets, but now has only eight, because poor wee Pluto got downgraded from proper planet to dwarf planet in 2006 (which is not that surprising when you consider that the surface area of Russia is greater than that of Pluto).

The eight planets of the solar system

Starting from the sun and working outwards, i.e. from Mercury to Neptune, the eight planets within the solar system are as follows:

Mercury

    Venus

        Earth

           Mars

              Jupiter

                  Saturn

                      Uranus

                          Neptune

Of the other seven planets in the solar system, only Mars shows much hope of providing a safe enough environment to land a human being on, because the temperatures on Mercury are too extreme, Venus is too poisonous and the other planets are too gaseous. However, scientists are not ruling out the possibility of two of Jupiter's moons (Ganymede and Europa) and one of Saturn's moons (Titan) being able to support human life.

STUFF AND NONSENSE

Only babies could live on Neptune

Because it takes Neptune 165 years to orbit the sun and therefore complete the equivalent of a single earth year, nobody would ever sing 'Happy Birthday' to you if you were born there, and you would never get a single birthday present and you would always be the same age as your mum and dad. On the plus side, there would be no generation gap to worry about.

Why on earth is there life on earth?

If Goldilocks had been sent to choose one of the eight planets of the solar system to live on, she would undoubtedly have chosen earth, because it is the only one that is 'just right' to sustain human life, primarily because it is just the right amount of distance (150 million km, or 93 million miles) away from the sun. Being just the right amount of distance from the sun ensures the correct amounts of heat, light and water that are necessary to produce a climate and atmosphere capable of supporting our existence. Generally speaking, we earthlings do not appreciate just how lucky we are to have a planet to live on, which is why we are really bad at looking after it, I suppose.

Moons

Of the eight planets in the solar system, six have moons of their own (only Mercury and Venus do not have moons). The earth has only one, of course, but some of the others have lots. Jupiter alone has over 60.

The moons of the other planets have been given brilliant names like Titan, Pandora, Calypso, Prospero and Triton. In order not to confuse our moon with their moons, we have called our moon 'the moon'. In spite of its rather unimaginative title, though, it performs a number of very important functions:

1. It stabilises the earth's rotation to the extent of keeping our seasons fairly regular, which is essential for the long-term evolution and sustainability of life.
2. Its gravity pulls at our oceans with a constant force, so that our sailors and fishermen know well in advance when our tides will come in and go out.

3. When it's reflecting light from the sun, it allows us to see a bit in the dark, especially at sea and in the countryside away from the light pollution of our towns and cities.
4. It allows many nocturnal animals and sea creatures to see well enough in the dark to migrate, mate, feed themselves and catch their prey.
5. Its rotation as a natural satellite gave scientists the idea that we could put artificial satellites into orbit as well, thereby giving us mobile telephones, wireless internet, satnav and satellite TV, including live sport from anywhere in the world.
6. It makes the night sky look nice.

GREAT ASTRONOMERS

People have, quite rightly, been fascinated by the sky since they first clapped eyes on it. They have continued to explore it in whatever ways they can, especially at night-time when the stars come out to play. Even searching the universe with the naked eye is not as limiting as you might think. Without a telescope on a clear night we can regularly see the Andromeda galaxy, 2.6 million light years from earth and therefore beyond our own Milky Way galaxy. Just keep your eye open for what looks like a star that is more smudged than the rest.

Let's have a look at some of the great astronomers who have looked at the sky a bit more carefully than that, though.

Galileo Galilei

The Italian astronomer Galileo Galilei has been dubbed the Father of Observational Astronomy because he was the first man, way back in the seventeenth century, to start to get a real handle on it. Amongst other things, he discovered the four largest moons of Jupiter, performed analysis of sunspots and confirmed the different phases of Venus, all with a fairly rudimentary telescope.

Edwin Hubble

The powerful telescopes available to American astronomer Edwin Hubble in the first half of the twentieth century allowed him to look deeper into the universe than ever before and to ascertain that fudgy-looking nebulae like Andromeda were in fact galaxies beyond our own. Until then, we had rather assumed that we were on our own, and that there was nothing beyond our little Milky Way.

Georges Lemaître

After serving as an artillery officer throughout the First World War, the versatile Belgian Georges Lemaître became a priest and studied mathematics, physics and astronomy. He studied so hard that he eventually established the Big Bang theory, which he in fact referred to as the primeval atom, or Cosmic Egg. Having established that other galaxies were moving ever faster and ever further away from our own, he applied a bit of reverse thinking to establish that these far-away galaxies used to be not very far away at all, and that they had all once exploded out of the same Cosmic Egg with the same Big Bang. Many of Lemaître's findings were published in an obscure journal, which later led to them being misattributed to Edwin Hubble, but the world knows better now.

STUFF AND NONSENSE

A lack of universal recognition

It troubles me somewhat that the man responsible for establishing the origins of the universe is not as universally (pun intended) recognised as fellow scientists like Albert Einstein or Isaac Newton. In fact, most people today are more familiar with popular science celebrities like Bill Nye, Brian Cox and Dara Ó Briain than they are with Georges Lemaître. On the plus side, Lemaître does have a few things named after him, including a small planet, a crater on the moon and a Norwegian indie electro band, but I still think the universe owes him a bit more respect than he gets.

Albert Einstein

Everybody knows that the German-born Nobel Prize-winning physicist was a genius who changed the world, but not everyone knows that he lost his bottle when it came to matters of the cosmos. His theory of relativity had established that massive objects like planets and stars warped (or bent) space-time to cause gravity, and this therefore suggested that the universe was either expanding or contracting. However, because the prevailing wisdom of the day was adamant that the universe was fixed and eternal, Einstein dropped a random 'cosmological constant' into his equations in order not to rock the boat too much. He later recognised this as his 'greatest blunder'.

Stephen Hawking

The most recognisable scientist of modern times, Hawking is lauded for popularising science by explaining difficult concepts in understandable ways. His work on black holes helped confirm the Big Bang theory, because black holes are a bit like the Big Bang in reverse. He has achieved a huge amount in spite of the motor neurone disease that has afflicted him since the age of 21, even finding time to squeeze in guest appearances on *Star Trek: The Next Generation* and *The Simpsons*.

THE EXPLORATION OF SPACE

It was only ever a matter of time before mankind got up close and personal with space, and that has been achieved, and continues to be achieved, through a remarkable series of telescopic, robotic and manned explorations.

Telescopic observation

Huge, powerful telescopes continue to capture the wonders of the universe from the surface of our planet, but even sharper images are available from those that have been launched into orbit. By way of example, in 1990 NASA launched the Hubble Space Telescope into orbit 550 km (342 miles) above earth. The size of a large bus, it continues even now to take sharp pictures of galaxies, stars and planets. It has captured the birth and death of stars and the crashing of comets into Jupiter's atmosphere, and it takes pictures of galaxies 10–15 billion light years away (it is estimated that the edge of the 'observable' universe is 46 billion light years away, so we still have some way to go before we can see out to the edge of the known universe).

Robotic spaceflight

Robotic spacecraft are generally controlled by one of the worldwide networks of large antennae and communication facilities that have been built to support interplanetary space missions, like the Deep Space Network run by NASA. Russia, China, Japan, India and Europe (in the form of the European Space Agency) have their own such networks. Unmanned space missions generally cost less and carry less risk than manned space missions, but mostly they come into their own to explore planets that are too hostile to support a human visit or that are too far away to reach with current manned spacecraft technology. Here are a few examples of the robotic explorations that have occurred to date:

1957	Sputnik 1 (USSR) became the first artificial satellite to orbit the earth
	Sputnik 2 (USSR) took the first living animal (a dog named Laika) into orbit
1958	First lunar flyby (USSR) – intended to impact the moon but missed
1962	Interplanetary space flight (USA) reached as far as Venus, the nearest planet to earth
1965	First flyby and close-up view of Mars (USA)
1966	USSR and USA achieved first soft landings on the moon
	First photographs from lunar surface (USA)
1970	Venus was the first planet to enjoy a soft landing by a spacecraft from earth (USSR)
	First rover deployed on lunar surface (USSR)
1971	Mars space probes (USA and USSR) sent pictures back from orbit
1975	First fully successful soft landing of lander module on Mars (USA)
1976	Solar probe came within 43 million km of the sun (USA and West Germany)
1989	First flyby of Neptune, the furthest planet in our solar system (USA)
1997	First successful deployment of Mars rover (USA)

| 2014 | Space probe Rosetta successfully landed on a comet after a ten-year journey from earth, via a Mars flyby (European Space Agency) |

Human spaceflight

Cosmonauts and astronauts

A cosmonaut is someone who has been trained and certified by the Russian Space Agency, while an astronaut is someone who has been trained and certified by any of the other main space agencies, including NASA and the European Space Agency. Here are just a few of their magnificent achievements, whatever we choose to call them:

1961	Yuri Gagarin (USSR) became the first man in space, completing one orbit in 1 hour 48 minutes and bailing out with a parachute following re-entry
1963	Valentina Tereshkova (USSR) became the first woman in space
1965	Aleksey Leonov (USSR) carried out the first 'spacewalk' when he went floating about for 12 minutes outside his spacecraft
1967	Vladimir Komarov was the first man to die on a space mission after the parachute on his spacecraft failed to open properly on his return to earth

1969	Neil Armstrong (USA) became the first man to walk on the moon
	Edwin 'Buzz' Aldrin (USA) became the second man to walk on the moon
	Michael Collins (USA) became the first man to fly to the moon and back (as the Apollo 11 pilot who dropped Neil Armstrong and Buzz Aldrin off)
1970	Apollo 13 (USA) suffered an explosion en route to the moon but was nursed safely back to earth without loss of life
1971	The first manned space station, Salyut 1, was launched into earth orbit (USSR)
	The first moon buggy was used by an astronaut to explore the surface of the moon (USA)
1972	Eugene Cernan (USA) became the eleventh person to walk on the moon, and the twelfth and last person (to date) to leave a footprint on the moon (because his crewmate, Harrison Schmitt, stepped onto the moon after him but then returned to the lunar module before him). In the absence of any weather on the moon, the footprints are all still there
1981	The first reusable spacecraft (Space Shuttle Columbia, USA) was launched with rockets and landed back on earth as a glider

1986	The Space Shuttle Challenger (USA) exploded shortly after take-off, killing all seven astronauts
1986–2000	104 different astronauts/cosmonauts from 12 different nations spent time aboard the Mir space station
1991	Helen Sharman became the first British person in space when she joined two Russians on an expedition to the Mir space station
1995	Russian cosmonaut Valery Polyakov completed a record 437 days in orbit
1998	36 years after he became the first American astronaut to orbit the earth, John Glenn, aged 77, became the oldest person to fly in space when he went up to the International Space Station so that they could conduct experiments on the impact of weightlessness, etc. on an older person
2000	The first 'permanent' crew moved into the International Space Station
2001	American engineer Dennis Tito became the first space tourist when he paid a reported $20 million for a return trip to the International Space Station
2003	Space Shuttle Columbia (USA) broke apart on re-entry, killing all seven astronauts on board

2016	While on a six-month mission to the International Space Station, Tim Peake became the first 'official' British astronaut to complete a spacewalk (the British-born astronaut Michael Foale had completed a spacewalk in 1995, but he was an American citizen by then and he flew as an American astronaut)

International Space Station (ISS)

In 1998, the ISS became the ninth space station to be inhabited by crews and replaced the Mir's functions as a research laboratory in earth orbit. It is the largest artificial satellite in earth orbit and can be seen from earth with the naked eye. In addition to scientific experiments, it is used to test systems and equipment required for missions to the moon and Mars. Here are some more cool facts about the ISS:

1. It maintains a height of 330–435 km (205–270 miles) above earth.
2. It completes 15.54 orbits of the earth per day.
3. It has been manned continuously since November 2000.
4. As of March 2016, it has been visited by 222 astronauts/cosmonauts and space tourists from 18 different countries, including 33 women.
5. Space tourists get to stay on the space station for a week or two while the outgoing crew hands over to the incoming one (it's important not to miss the shuttle home because there won't be another one for a while).

6. English singer Sarah Brightman was due to pay $52 million to be the eighth space tourist to visit the station in 2015 but changed her mind.

7. Russian cosmonaut Yuri Malenchenko has made the most visits to the ISS (five).

8. Malenchenko also became the first person to marry in space in 2003 – at the time of the ceremony his bride was in Texas and he was 386 km (240 miles) over New Zealand.

Tim Peake

The ex-army helicopter pilot beat 9,000 other hopefuls to be accepted into the European Space Agency and was selected for a mission to the International Space Station in 2015 after intensive training as an astronaut. Social media coupled with satellite technology (I'm guessing the signal is quite good up there) has allowed him to communicate regularly with British earthlings, including a New Year's message broadcast by the BBC and a video link to present British singer Adele with her BRIT award for Global Success.

He hitched a lift to the space station with a Russian cosmonaut and an American astronaut on a Soyuz spacecraft and, in accordance with tradition, he was allowed three songs to listen to during the launch. These are the songs he chose:

'Don't Stop Me Now'	Queen
'Beautiful Day'	U2
'A Sky Full of Stars'	Coldplay

To infinity and beyond

We can never be sure what the future holds, but there seems little doubt that the human race will explore further into space, and that space tourism will become an increasingly regular occurrence for those that can afford it. It only takes three days to get to the moon as it is, and US space policy already has a stated objective to send humans to orbit Mars in the 2030s. Using current technology, it would take around 18–24 months to get to Mars and back, but we all know what happens to current technology. Who is to say that we won't soon have bases on the moon and on Mars as stepping stones to wherever we're going to end up one day, or that colonisation of other planets or moons is out of the question? It's not that long ago that the world was flat, don't forget.

Astrology

It is important not to confuse astronomy with astrology, as the latter concerns itself solely with how the position of other planets and stars affect our lives here on earth. For thousands of years, people have interpreted the position of celestial bodies as everything from divine intervention to the many systems of horoscopes that exist to establish the personality traits of individuals and to forecast their future significant events. It may be a bit of fun to some, and it is still taken very seriously by others, but, one way or another, it's not rocket science!

THIS SPORTING
WORLD

INTRODUCTION

After all that difficult stuff about science, technology and the universe, I think we should treat ourselves to some sporting trivia to finish off with. Don't worry if you're not that into sport, because this is going to be pretty light-hearted stuff. Let's have an irreverent look at some of the world's most important sports, starting with Muggle Quidditch.

QUIDDITCH

There are around 700 officially recognised sports in the world, including a gender-neutral version of Quidditch based on the game played at Hogwarts in the Harry Potter novels (in other words, what Harry would refer to as Muggle Quidditch). An international federation and 18 national governing bodies around the world ensure that the game is played according to the rules, which include the following:

1. All seven team members on each side must have a broomstick between their legs at all times.
2. Each team must have no more than four players who identify as the same gender.
3. Goals are scored by passing the quaffle ball through the goal hoop of the opposing team.
4. Any player hit by a beater's bludger is out of play until they next touch their own team's goal hoop.

5.   The snitch (a tennis ball in a long sock) will be attached to the waistband of a neutral runner dressed in yellow, who will try to avoid capture during the match.

6.   The game is over when a team's seeker catches the snitch.

OLYMPIC STUFF

Second only to Muggle Quidditch in capturing the public imagination, the Olympics have been throwing up sporting heroes and cool anecdotes since the Modern Games started up in Athens in 1896. The main difference between the Ancient Games and the Modern Games is that the athletes get to keep their clothes on nowadays (*gymnos* is the Greek word for naked, in fact, so next time you go to the gym try asserting your linguistic right to hit the running machine as god intended you should). Here are some cool facts to keep you going until the next Winter or Summer Games come around:

The '100-metre freestyle for sailors' swimming event took place at the 1896 Athens Olympics. It was only open to sailors of the Greek Royal Navy and, perhaps unsurprisingly, Greece took the gold, silver and bronze medals.

The youngest winner of an Olympic medal was Dimitrios Loundros, a ten year-old Greek gymnast who won bronze at the 1896 Athens Olympics, and the oldest winner was Swedish marksman Oscar Swahn, who won a shooting silver medal at the age of 72 at the Antwerp Games in 1920.

In the 1928 Amsterdam Olympics, Australian rower Henry Pearce stopped to let a family of ducks cross his lane and still won the gold medal.

Painting, sculpture, architecture, literature and music were Olympic events from 1912 to 1948. Jack Yeats, the brother of poet W. B. Yeats, took the painting silver medal at Paris in 1924 to win Ireland's first ever Olympic medal.

Other ex-Olympic events include the following worthy (and one not-so-worthy) sports:

1. standing high jump
2. tug of war
3. two-handed javelin
4. tandem cycling
5. underwater swimming
6. equestrian long jump
7. croquet
8. one-handed weightlifting
9. solo synchronised swimming (as recently as 1992)
10. obstacle swimming race (which involved scrambling over and under rows of boats)
11. duelling pistols (using human silhouettes dressed in frock coats as the targets)
12. live pigeon shooting (nearly 400 birds were killed within a small area and the resulting scene was one of carnage)

The Paralympics are the second-largest multi-sport competition in the world after the Olympics, with over 4,000 athletes representing over 160 countries (compared to around 11,000 atheletes from around 190 countries at the Olympics). The word Paralympics comes from the Greek for beside (*para*) Olympics, hence they are the 'parallel games'.

Dutch wheelchair tennis legend Esther Vergeer retired in 2013 after 470 straight wins that included four Paralympic gold-medal victories.

The Spanish Paralympic basketball team that won gold at the Sydney games in 2000 later had to hand their medals back, after ten of them were found not to have a disability.

The Winter Olympics are literally way cooler than the Summer Olympics and Norway is the coolest competing country by a long way, with 329 medals and counting, including the record-breaking 12 won by their cross-country skier Bjørn Dæhlie.

American swimmer Michael Phelps, aka the 'Flying Fish', is the most-decorated Olympian of all time, with 23 gold medals alone, which is 14 more than anyone else in history.

About 450,000 condoms were made available to athletes competing in the 2016 Rio de Janeiro Olympics – three times more than during the 2012 London Games. They included about 100,000 female condoms, which were made available for the first time.

FOOTBALL STUFF

Much more important than life or death according to Liverpool's legendary manager Bill Shankly, football has become a billion-pound industry across the globe, with players and managers changing clubs for ludicrous sums of money and referees facing an impossible task to control the antics of prima donna footballers who will stop at nothing to achieve the glory that awaits every goal or victory. When played well, though, it remains the most beautiful game in the eyes of its worldwide followers:

The Kop (short for Spion Kop) stand at various English football grounds, most famously at Anfield, home of Liverpool FC, was so named after the mound on which the Battle of Spion Kop (1900) was fought in the Second Boer War in South Africa. This was because the original standing-only terrace at these football grounds was built on a similar-looking natural mound overlooking the pitch. *Spion* translates from Afrikaans as 'spy' or 'lookout' and *kop* translates as 'hill' or 'outcrop'.

The first televised football in Britain was a specially arranged match behind closed doors for the BBC between Arsenal and Arsenal Reserves in 1937. No record of the result survives but I like to think the wee team beat the big team.

In 1978 the Sheffield United manager Harry Haslam went on a scouting trip to Argentina, where a young lad by the name of Diego Maradona took his eye. A transfer fee of £200,000 was agreed but the Sheffield United board refused to stump up all the required money and the deal fell through. Bad mistake.

In the 48 hours following England's loss to Argentina in a World Cup penalty shoot-out in 1998, the number of heart attacks in England went up by 25 per cent.

In 2002, in protest against refereeing decisions that had gone against them in earlier matches, a league team in Madagascar lost 149–0 to their main rivals by scoring 149 own goals, barely letting their opponents touch the ball.

The San Marino international football team has only ever won one match (out of 134 at the time of writing), which was a 1–0 victory in a friendly against Liechtenstein in 2004. It has never won a competitive match, but it does hold the record for scoring the fastest World Cup goal in history, after just 8.3 seconds in a World Cup qualifier against England.

In 2007 Leroy Rosenior was unveiled as the new manager of Torquay United, telling the assembled press that he looked forward to bringing some much-needed stability to the club. The club was taken over during the press conference and the new owners ended the much-needed stability that Rosenior brought to the club after a reign of just ten minutes – the shortest managerial tenure on record.

Over ten per cent of the 49,000-strong population of the remote Faroe Islands are registered to play in one of the many junior, men's or women's football leagues. Playing conditions are usually pretty tough. On one ground, perched on the edge of the Atlantic, the players sometimes have to lie down flat until the wind abates enough for them to continue. If the wind carries the ball out to sea, there are fishermen waiting on rowing boats on the choppy ocean to retrieve it.

In 2016 Leicester City achieved the seemingly impossible task of winning the English Premier League within 13 months of being bottom of the table towards the end of the previous season. Thanks to the managerial magic that the personable Italian Claudio Ranieri brought to the club, they did this without any well-known stars or big-money signings.

NORTH AMERICAN STUFF

Across the pond, our American cousins continue to do the old sporting razzmatazz far better than anyone else can ever hope to achieve. Just don't say you're a big football fan if you mean soccer, and don't go to a hockey match if sport on dry land is your thing. For jolly hockey sticks, read body smash on ice:

The average playing time in an American football game of four quarters (i.e. one hour) is about 12 minutes, leaving about three hours including the breaks for hot dogs and cheerleading.

The basketball court on the fifth floor of the Supreme Court building in Washington, D.C. is known as the highest court in the land.

Legendary (ice) hockey injuries have included a goalie set on fire when the puck struck a box of matches he had in his pocket; a player's jugular vein being split open by an errant stick (the player survived after his trainer reached into his neck and pinched off the bleeding until medics arrived); a spectator being beaten with his own shoe after a player took exception to something he shouted out; and a bat that got mistaken (fatally) for the puck when it flew across the ice.

In 2000, Pope John Paul II was made an honorary Harlem Globetrotter basketball player when the team visited him at the Vatican, although ice hockey and skiing were his sports of choice while growing up in Poland.

American basketball player Michael Jordan made more money in sponsorship from Nike in a year than all the Nike factory workers in Malaysia combined.

Baseball may be the USA's national sport, but it is also the most popular sport in Japan. At international level, Japan is ranked number one ahead of the USA and Chinese Taipei.

Cheerleading causes more serious injuries to women in the USA than any other sport.

TENNIS STUFF

It may be popular all over the world, but tennis fever grips Britain like nowhere else when the signs go up in SW19 each summer for the Wimbledon Championships. Half a million people attend the tournament, consuming 27,000 kg of strawberries and 7,000 litres of cream in the process, while millions of others remain glued to their TV screens every chance they get. Here are some tennis facts to keep you going until the next big tournament comes your way:

The fastest recorded serve in men's tennis is 163.7 mph by the Australian Sam Groth in 2012, and the fastest recorded serve in women's tennis is 131 mph by the German Sabine Lisicki in 2014.

In 2008 a newspaper branded Britain's Robert Dee 'the world's worst professional tennis player' after he lost 54 matches in a row on the international circuit without winning a single set. He took the newspaper to court, only to have the judge confirm that he was indeed the world's worst professional tennis player.

The longest professional tennis match on record was at Wimbledon in 2010, when the 6 ft 10 in American John Isner finally defeated Frenchman Nicolas Mahut 6–4, 3–6, 6–7, 7–6, 70–68 after 11 hours and 5 minutes over three days. Isner served 113 aces and Mahut served 103. The following day, an exhausted Isner lost his second-round match in straight sets without serving a single ace.

Nobody is entirely sure why 'love' is used instead of 'nil' or 'zero' in tennis scoring, but the most popular theory is that it came from the French *l'oeuf*, because the number 0 very much resembles an egg, *n'est-ce pas*? A more linguistically correct scoring system would therefore include 15–egg, 30–egg and 40–egg. The reasons for 15, 30 and 40 being used are apparently lost in the mists of the French language.

The venue used for the French Open is named after French First World War fighter pilot Roland Garros, who was instrumental in developing a machine gun that could be fired through an aeroplane's propeller, allowing him to serve a complete volley of shots at the oncoming enemy planes.

Research has shown that grunting, shrieking and squealing at the point of playing a tennis shot increases the ball's velocity by around 4 per cent, which is over 5 mph for the top players. No research has been necessary to establish that it makes the player in question sound like a Neanderthal halfwit or that it is extremely annoying to their opponents and spectators alike.

Swiss player Roger Federer is the greatest male tennis player of all time, with 17 Grand Slams, three more than American Pete Sampras and Spaniard Rafael Nadal. He held the world number 1 position for 302 weeks (including 237 consecutive weeks) – 15 more than Sampras.

Australian Margaret Court is the most successful female player of all time, with 24 Grand Slam victories, two more at the time of writing than both the German Steffi Graf and the American Serena Williams.

Goran Ivanišević is the only Wimbledon champion with a name that alternates vowels and consonants.

GOLF STUFF

Ever since James VI of Scotland also became James I of England in 1603 and brought his court and all their golf clubs down south to London with him, golf has continued to spread across the globe. At the time of writing, there are 34,011 courses in 206 countries, with a combined total of 576,534 holes you'll have to conquer before you can call yourself the complete golfer. Here are some cool facts to impress your golfing buddies with on your next round:

When American astronaut Alan Shepard played two six-iron shots on the moon in 1971, one ball went into orbit and the other ended up in a crater, making it the only hole-in-one recorded on the lunar surface to date.

Chairman Mao banned golf in 1949, declaring it too bourgeois for Communist China. The ban was lifted in the 1980s but in 2004 the construction of new golf courses was made illegal due to concerns over 'environmental damage'. In 2015 President Xi Jinping effectively banned all 88 million members of the ruling Communist Party of China from joining golf clubs when he prohibited them from accepting memberships as gifts or using public funds, because he considered golf clubs to be ideal places to discuss suspect deals.

The game has been popular in North Korea ever since Kim Jong-il played his one and only game of golf in 1994 and scored a remarkable 38-under-par round of 34 that included 11 holes-in-one. That was according to his official biography, so I assume it must be true.

Japanese golfers take out insurance against the risk of getting a hole-in-one, because tradition dictates that they should celebrate the unlikely event by throwing a party complete with significant gifts for all their friends. It is estimated that around 4 million golfers in the country take out policies at a cost of around £50 per annum to guard against the, statistically speaking, 12,000 to 1 chance that a hole-in-one will be achieved.

Appropriately enough for the home of golf, Scotland has more golf courses per capita than any other country, followed by Ireland, New Zealand and Australia.

The most successful men's golfer of all time is the American Jack Nicklaus, with 18 major championships – four more at the time of writing than fellow American Tiger Woods.

Tiger Woods' real name is Eldrick Tont Woods.

The most successful women's golfer of all time is the American Patty Berg, with 15 major championships, and it would have been more had she not taken time off to serve as a lieutenant in the Marines during the Second World War and to recover from a shattered knee suffered during a head-on collision in a car.

CRICKET STUFF

More than just a game, cricket is considered by many to be the blueprint for the rules of life, ensuring fair play and a stiff upper lip in the face of defeat. It's just not cricket to be a bad sport or to fail to appreciate the sterling efforts of the chaps on the other team. Try these facts out in the pavilion the next time rain stops play:

The Test-match batting average of 99.94 achieved by Australian batsman Don Bradman is considered by many to be the finest achievement of any sportsman in any sport. It would have been 100 had he scored just 4 runs in his final innings at the Oval in 1948, but he was instead bowled out for a duck by the second ball he faced.

Sri Lankan fast bowler Muttiah Muralitharan holds the record for wickets taken in Test matches (800) and One Day Internationals (534). He took his

800th and last Test wicket with his last ball in his last Test match. That's what you call an exit, Mr Bradman.

Indian batsman Sachin Tendulkar scored more Test runs (15,921) than anyone else in history, followed by the Australian Ricky Ponting (13,378).

Trinidadian batsman Brian Lara holds the record for most runs scored in a first-class innings (501) and in a Test-match innings (400 not out).

The Allahakbarries were an amateur cricket team founded by *Peter Pan* author J. M. Barrie in 1890. Other notable authors roped into the team included H. G. Wells, Jerome K. Jerome, Arthur Conan Doyle, Rudyard Kipling, A. A. Milne and P. G. Wodehouse. Barrie also commandeered explorers, soldiers, actors, an international footballer and a missionary to play for him.

Julius Caesar was a first-class cricketer for Surrey in the late nineteenth century. His father was a professional cricketer and his mother's maiden name was Bowler, so he was destined from the off to be a bit of an all-rounder. However, he went on to underachieve somewhat, with a below-average batting average of 15.78 and a decent-enough bowling average of 23.62 (although he never really bowled that much), resulting in a few less 'Hail Caesars' than his parents probably wished for when they chose his name.

RUGBY STUFF

Ever since young William Webb Ellis supposedly picked up the ball and ran with it during a football match at Rugby School in 1823, the game of rugby has been putting football to shame with its lack of player histrionics coupled with total respect for the authority of the referee. It can be a difficult game to follow, though, so here is some stuff you should know whether you are a diehard fan or whether you count yourself amongst those uninitiated observers who don't understand why a try is called a try:

Originally, a try had no value. It simply allowed an attacking team that had breached the defence of the opposing team to 'try' a kick between the posts. If the 'try' was 'converted', it became a goal.

Scotland beat England 1–0 in the first international rugby union match ever played, in 1871 in Edinburgh, having converted one try at goal. In total, Scotland had just two tries at goal throughout the entire match, and England had just one.

The population of the English town of Rugby in Warwickshire is not sufficient to fill the home of English rugby, Twickenham Stadium.

The USA were the reigning Olympic rugby champions from 1924 – the last time rugby was an Olympic sport, as 15-a-side rugby union in Paris – until

2016, when rugby was reintroduced at the Rio de Janeiro Olympics, this time as rugby sevens.

The wife of the man who made rugby balls for Rugby School in the nineteenth century died after inhaling too much poison from the pig bladders used to make the balls (it was her job to blow them up using nothing but her own puff).

The trophy awarded to the winner of the annual rugby union match between Scotland and England (currently played as one of the fixtures of the Six Nations Championship) is the Calcutta Cup, which is made from melted-down Indian rupees and decorated with cobras and an elephant. It has been in a fragile state of repair since 1988, when two drunken players (one from each side) played rugby with it along Princes Street in Edinburgh following the after-match dinner. In order to preserve the original, a replica trophy is now presented to the winning team each year.

Rugby league is a breakaway form of rugby union, played at a faster pace with fewer players (13 a side as opposed to 15-a-side) and with faster restarts after play has broken down. On average, the ball is in play for 50 out of 80 minutes in a rugby league match and for 35 out of 80 minutes in a rugby union match.

England dominates women's rugby, having won the World Cup in 2014 and regularly topping the Six Nations table. Around 20,000 women now play the game at various levels across the country.

CYCLING STUFF

Cycling has become huge again in recent years as people around the world look to get themselves fitter and want to care for their planet a bit better. In Britain in particular, the popularity of cycling at every level has exploded following the running of some Tour de France stages in England and the resulting success of the fledgling Tour de Yorkshire (which held its inaugural race in 2016 and had over a million people lining the roads to cheer on the competitors). Here are some cool facts to get you fired up enough to join the current revolution (pun intended):

The Belgian racer Eddy Merckx remains the best road racer the world has ever seen, having dominated road racing for ten years from 1966 onwards, winning a record 11 Grand Tours (five Tour de France, five Giro d'Italia and one Vuelta a España) and all five Monuments of Cycling (Milan–San Remo, Tour of Flanders, Paris–Roubaix, Liège–Bastogne–Liège and Giro di Lombardia). He was nicknamed 'the Cannibal' in view of his insatiable appetite for eating up miles.

The versatile Dutchwoman Marianne Vos is the most successful female bike racer in history, having excelled as a world champion in four different cycling disciplines (road, track, mountain bike and cyclo-cross). She was world cyclo-cross champion and world road-racing champion by the time she was 19 and she went on to win two Olympic gold medals, one on the track and one on the road.

British track cyclists Chris Hoy and Jason Kenny are the most successful Olympic cyclists of all time, with six gold medals and one silver each. That also makes them the most successful British Olympians of all time.

Fellow British cyclist Bradley Wiggins is just behind Chris Hoy and Jason Kenny in terms of Olympic success, having taken five gold, one silver and two bronze medals, but he also went on to win the Tour de France – a very different type of race requiring a totally different training regime in order to achieve the fitness and physique of an endurance athlete.

The most successful bike racer in Tour de France history was the American Lance Armstrong, until it was finally established in 2012 that he had taken performance-enhancing drugs throughout his career. His seven consecutive victories between 1999 and 2005 have been stripped from the record book.

In the second ever Tour de France in 1904, many of the competitors were disqualified for jumping on trains or taking lifts in cars during the night.

The Dutch use their bicycles for one in three of all journeys made, compared to one in a hundred in the USA.

The number of bicycles and cars in the world are both over a billion, but twice as many new bicycles are now being made each year than cars.

Famous unicyclists include Formula One drivers Lewis Hamilton and Nico Rosberg, actor Rupert Grint (Ron Weasley in the Harry Potter films), the Take That band members (past and present) Howard Donald, Jason Orange and Mark Owen, Coldplay lead man Chris Martin and former US Secretary of Defence Donald Rumsfeld.

RUNNING STUFF

Running maintains its popularity for the purposes of recreation, keeping fit or the need to prove something to yourself over a distance of 26 miles and 385 yards. The most important lesson that you learn from running this marathon distance, of course, is that it really hurts to run non-stop for 26 miles and 385 yards. The second most important lesson is that you shouldn't do it again unless you want to hurt yourself again. Here are some thoughts to keep your mind off the pain the next time you're out there doing it:

English runner Roger Bannister broke the four-minute barrier on 6 May 1954, when he ran the mile at Oxford University's Iffley Road Track in 3 minutes 59.4 seconds. He only held the world record for 46 days, though, before the Australian John Landy recorded a time of 3 minutes 58 seconds at a race in Finland.

New Yorker Jim Fixx is credited with kick-starting the fitness revolution with his best-selling *The Complete Book of Running*. He died at the age of 52, while out running.

English runner Paula Radcliffe remains the women's marathon world record holder at the time of writing, having set a time of 2 hours 15 minutes 25 seconds way back in the 2003 London Marathon. The men's world record is 2 hours 2 minutes 57 seconds, set by Kenyan Dennis Kimetto in Berlin in 2014.

Jamaican sprinter Usain Bolt is the fastest person on the planet, but his first love was cricket. During a charity match, he clean-bowled fellow-Jamaican cricket legend Chris Gayle and then hit a six when it was Gayle's turn to bowl at him.

The London Marathon is the largest annual one-day fundraising event in the world. It has raised around £800 million since it began in 1981, and some people will stop at nothing to raise funds for their chosen causes. At the 2016 London Marathon alone, new world records were established for the following:

1. Fastest marathon dressed as an elf (male)
2. Fastest marathon dressed as a book character (female) (she chose Tinker Bell from J. M. Barrie's *Peter Pan*)
3. Fastest marathon dressed as a tap (male)

4. Fastest marathon in a film-character costume (male) (but he ran as Elsa from *Frozen*)
5. Fastest marathon as a fast-food product (he ran as a hotdog)
6. Fastest marathon as a crustacean (in spite of running as a lobster and having a tendency to trip over his own tail, he ran the race in just over 3 hours)
7. Fastest marathon in an animal costume (female) (recorded a time of 03:19:41 as a tortoise, which is very fast indeed for a tortoise)
8. Fastest marathon in a full-body animal costume (female) (she ran as a polar bear)
9. Fastest marathon as a bottle (male) (it was a full-length mock-up of a bottle of Wimbledon Brewery's Tower Special Pale Ale)
10. Fastest marathon in a ghillie suit (a ghillie is a camouflage suit, but this one obviously wasn't very effective, because if it had been no one would have found the woman concerned to award her a well-earned Guinness World Record certificate)
11. Fastest marathon dressed as a plant (he ran as a flower pot)
12. Fastest marathon dressed as an internal organ (he ran as a prostate)
13. Fastest marathon dressed as a gingerbread man
14. Fastest marathon dressed as an astronaut (male)
15. Fastest marathon run as an actual astronaut in earth orbit (this was Tim Peake on a treadmill in the International Space Station)

In 2013 Jake Harrison of Leicester had such a big lead coming to the end of the Marathon of the North in Sunderland that he was literally out of sight of the runners behind him. When the runners in second and third place took a wrong turning, the race marshals didn't notice and everyone else in the 5,000-strong field followed suit. They all found their way back to the correct route soon enough, but they had taken a shortcut that resulted in them all running 264 metres short of the full marathon distance. Months of punishing training and hours of gruelling racing left many of them where they had started the day – never having completed a marathon.

SOME RANDOM SPORT STUFF TO FINISH WITH

In ancient Mayan ball games, some or all of the losing team were decapitated in a ritual sacrifice to the gods. 'Shall we make it the best of three matches?' were the commonest final words uttered by members of the losing team.

In 1974, in order to make the Queen's visit more interesting, the British administration in Vanuatu convinced some villagers to 'land dive' (the precursor of bungee jumping but using vines from the forest instead of ropes) for her entertainment. As it was the wet season, the vines were not always sufficiently elastic to break the fall of the contestants and Her Majesty watched on in horror as the vines snapped and a villager plummeted to his death.

The oldest continuous competition in sport is the America's Cup, held annually between two ocean-going sailing yachts. America won the trophy for a straight 132 years until Australia won in 1983.

At one time racecourse owners in Britain were so desperate for sponsorship that jockeys had to compete for the likes of the Mr Chris Real Dairy Cream Cake Handicap Hurdle, but there are worse things than winning the Mr Chris Real Dairy Cream Cake Handicap Hurdle – like coming last in the Mr Chris Real Dairy Cream Cake Handicap Hurdle.

While riding Central House in the Paddy Power Dial-A-Bet Chase at Leopardstown in 2005, jockey Roger Loughran celebrated victory by standing up in his stirrups, punching the air and waving to an unusually delirious crowd with his whip. Unfortunately, he had mistaken an upright bundle of birch for the finishing post and two other horses passed him before the real finishing line 100 yards further on.

Netball has long since been the most popular sport for females in Australia, with over a million participants, but it is now in danger of being overtaken by women's soccer.

The national game of Afghanistan is polo, except the ball is a headless goat carcass. The Afghans have been introducing more rules in recent times in the hope of getting goat-grabbing, or *buzkashi*, accepted as an Olympic sport.

CONCLUSION

I read somewhere that we can only retain ten per cent of what we read, but that we can increase our retention level to as much as 90 per cent by immediately putting into practice what we have learnt. The problem we have here is that putting into practice what you have learnt in this book is going to involve you travelling through time, visiting the far-flung corners of the earth, conquering vast swathes of land with a marauding army at your back and flying by Mars, to name but a few of the activities required to make the totality of the information sink in.

The only other thing I can suggest is reading the book another nine times, until you have arrived at 100 per cent assimilation, otherwise you'll just have to accept that you've already forgotten most of it. Maybe just keep it handy for future reference in that case. In any event, I hope you have enjoyed broadening your knowledge, however briefly.

If it's any consolation, I have already forgotten 90 per cent of what I just wrote by way of conclusion. Something about conquering Mars, I think.

A PLACE TO NOTE DOWN YOUR FAVOURITE STUFF

....
....
....
....
....
....
....
....
....
....
....
....
....
....
....
....
....
....

GRAMMAR

KNOW YOUR SHIT OR KNOW YOU'RE SHIT

JOANNE ADAMS

GRAMMAR
Know Your Shit or Know You're Shit

Joanne Adams

ISBN: 978-1-84953-757-5

Hardback

£7.99

'Let's eat Grandma'
OR
'Let's eat, Grandma'?

This fun yet informative book offers bite-sized tips and advice on everything you need to know about grammar – including common misspellings, how to use punctuation correctly and applying the right tense – and will turn you from a logophobe to a grammarphile in no time!

If you're interested in finding out more about our books, find us on Facebook at Summersdale Publishers and follow us on Twitter at @Summersdale.

www.summersdale.com